The Global Currencies Conundrum

THE GLOBAL CURRENCIES CONUNDRUM

Edited by John Ryan

PETER LANG
Oxford • Bern • Berlin • Bruxelles • Frankfurt am Main • New York • Wien

Bibliographic information published by Die Deutsche Nationalbibliothek
Die Deutsche Nationalbibliothek lists this publication in the Deutsche Nationalbibliografie; detailed bibliographic data is available on the Internet at http://dnb.d-nb.de.

A catalogue record for this book is available from the British Library.

Library of Congress Control Number: 2014946249

ISBN 978-3-0343-1767-2 (print)
ISBN 978-3-0353-0653-8 (eBook)

Hochfeldstrasse 32, CH-3012 Bern, Switzerland
info@peterlang.com, www.peterlang.com, www.peterlang.net

This publication has been peer reviewed.

Printed in Germany

Contents

Introduction

This book discusses the emergence of a multi-polar currency system.

The first chapter examines the implications of the creation of the Euro and its role as a global currency in today's multi-polar system of reserve currencies. In *'Currency Wars' Between the US and China: Has Europe Enough Monetary Power to Act as a Broker?*, Professor Otero-Iglesias discusses the role of the single currency not only as a reserve currency in a multi-polar system, but also as a real contender against the US Dollar's hegemony. Professor Otero-Iglesias discerns where the Eurozone stands within the current framework of increased 'currency wars' between the US and China, and whether it is able and willing to change the current International Monetary System to a more coordinated and managed exchange rate regime, as repeatedly stated. Professor Otero-Iglesias argues that the Eurozone has made certain progress in preference-shaping and agenda-setting, but not in decision-making which is still cumbersome. France, for instance, has certainly made some efforts, with the support of China, to start the debate on the transformation of the current Flexible-Dollar-Standard. However, by not being politically united, the Eurozone precludes any possibility to force the US to enter into a compromise and relinquish the 'exorbitant privilege' that the centrality of the Dollar offers them.

The second chapter examines *The Role of the Euro as a Global Currency after the 2008 crisis*. Professor Rinaldi investigates to what extent the 2008 crisis and its follow up has undermined the Euro's emerging international reserve currency status and examines whether there was enough real convergence between Eurozone economies before 2008 and draws lessons on the optimality of the European Monetary Union (EMU). It also analyses reforms proposed to tackle the sovereign debt crisis in terms of surveillance and governance rules, and questions its impact on the international role of the Euro. Through a first part devoted to the analysis of business cycles evolution since the launch of the European single currency, it will determine whether the criteria of the Optimum Currency Area theory were fulfilled by the Eurozone until 2008; then the chapter goes on to analyse the impact of the financial and economic crisis on Eurozone members, from an internal angle (has the Euro protected the Eurozone economies, or not, and in which respect?), as well as from an external angle (has the Euro been affected in its international role as a global currency by the crisis, or by the way the crisis was dealt with by member states and European institutions?). Reforms in European governance and the creation of tools needed to supervise the European banking and financial system and to reinforce the surveillance of budgetary positions in member states are examined. Scenarios of future developments of the sovereign debt crisis are then discussed, as well as pros and cons of exiting the Eurozone, especially for debt-laden countries. Finally, as a lesson of this crisis, how should European governance evolve in the near future?

In the third chapter, *China and the Global Role of Currencies*, Professor Ryan examines four scenarios regarding the global currency regime of the future and the Chinese influence in this most important policy arena. The focus is on the US Dollar decline as the Reserve Currency, on the Euro, on the potential of the Renminbi to become a Reserve Currency, and on the IMF's Special Drawing Rights (SDRs). The projected speed at which the Dollar will lose its predominant position as a global reserve currency depends on the US Treasury fiscal policy. Chinese and European leaders frequently emphasise the US responsibilities for the stability of the Dollar as the premier reserve currency. It is unclear whether the diversification benefit would be enough to make reserve managers willing to hold SDRs instead of Dollars (or Euros), unless the SDR takes a prominent role as unit of account or medium of exchange in global trade and financial transactions. The use of an SDR in international trade and finance would only come about slowly. China is actively engaged with Eurozone governments and EU institutions, and the latter have courted and welcomed Chinese intervention in financial markets, setting in motion an active monetary diplomacy. The preservation of the Euro has become not only a major EU objective, but it is also instrumental for Chinese leaders to achieve two overarching policy-goals: the internationalisation of the Renmimbi and the emergence of a multi-polar monetary order.

The fourth chapter examines *The Battle for the Euro! China's (Information) Strategy to Steer Market Sentiment in Favour of the Single Currency*. Professor Otero-Iglesias presents a detailed recompilation of China's informational and actual support for the Euro since its creation until present days. It will show how Chinese policymakers stepped in to sustain the value of the European currency every time it was under considerable market pressure during the 2010–12 Eurozone sovereign debt crisis. The strategy has been two-fold. On the one hand, the Chinese leadership has used public statements or commentaries in the state-owned media to show their confidence in the single currency, and on the other, they have accelerated their diversification moves out of the US Dollar and into the Euro. China's behaviour has changed market perceptions of the Euro, as recognised by financial heavy weights such as George Soros, who does not shy away from claiming that China effectively saved the Euro. The second part of this chapter is more analytical. The main aim is to explain why China is supporting the Euro and the European integration project at large. Several reasons are explored. China needs to diversify out of the Dollar, so this is a good opportunity to accelerate this process. China has already over $800bn in Euro-denominated assets; hence it needs to protect the value of its assets. The EU is China's most important market. Therefore it is in China's own national interest to stabilise the European market. Finally, this crisis is a good opportunity for China to present itself in front of its European counterparts as a reliable and trustworthy partner and consequently it should be granted market economy status and more saying in global economic and financial affairs.

In the final chapter, *Alan Greenspan and the Decline of the Federal Reserve's Dollar Policy*, Professor Ryan examines the US Dollar and its position as the closest thing to a true global currency that the world has seen. For decades, the use of the Dollar has absolutely dominated in international trade. This has had tremendous benefits for the US financial system and for US consumers, and it has given the US government tremendous power and influence around the globe. But there are big changes on the horizon. That privilege now is not only 'exorbitant' but 'extortionate'. How long the rest of the world will allow the US to exercise this extortionate privilege is uncertain. Leading politicians have been very critical of the

Federal Reserve having ominous powers that Congress barely understands and that trillions of Dollars can be created and injected into the economy with no obligation by the Federal Reserve to reveal who benefits. The Dollar depreciation has been blamed on the Greenspan and Bernanke Federal Reserve which has imposed an unwanted monetary system that is beneficial for Wall Street only.

MIGUEL OTERO-IGLESIAS

1 'Currency Wars' Between the US and China: Has Europe Enough Monetary Power to Act as a Broker?

Introduction

Similarly to the end of the 1960s, when the Bretton Woods system collapsed, and the 1980s, when the twin deficits of the US were also skyrocketing, in recent times (especially after the 'Wall Street Meltdown' in 2008) there is an increasing debate among International Political Economy (IPE) scholars on whether the centrality of the Dollar in the international monetary system (IMS) is in doubt (Helleiner & Kirshner 2009; Cohen 2010; Eichengreen 2011). The arguments of the current debate have similar features to earlier disputes on Dollar hegemony, while there are now new variables that make this discussion different. Where in the past there was Giscard d'Estaing and Charles de Gaulle complaining about the 'exorbitant privilege' enjoyed by the US, today we have Zhou Xiaochuan (2009), governor of the Chinese central bank (PBoC), and Hu Jintao, president of China, stating similar criticisms, pointing to the instabilities associated to the Triffin dilemma[1] and proposing, as was the case in the late 1960s with

1 As Triffin (1960) argued in the 1960s, the Dollar-standard suffers from one inherent flaw. By being based on a national currency, the issuer of the international currency, in this case the US, needs to run consistently large current account deficits to provide to the rest of the world the necessary liquidity for economic activity. However, the bloating of these deficits (essentially the misuse of the exorbitant privilege) undermines in the long term the credibility of the international currency and threatens with the collapse of the whole system (Bénassy-Quéré & Pisani-Ferry 2011).

the Europeans (Eichengreen 2008), an increased use of the Special Drawing Rights (SDRs) issued by the International Monetary Fund (IMF). The perceived rise of China as an upcoming world superpower is also comparable with the rise of Japan in the 1980s. China has also developed a successful export-led growth strategy, based in part on a devalued currency, which is said to be threatening the world's number one position of the US economy.

Seen from this light, the current debate about the demise of the Dollar seems overblown. Calls warning about the arrival of the wolf have been constant, but they have never materialised. As Susan Strange (1987) wrote in the late 1980s there seems to be a persistent myth surrounding the potential loss of US hegemony. Nonetheless, there are several important changes in the present IMS that make the current conjuncture different. Unlike in the 1960s and 1980s, today, with the consolidation of the Euro, the Dollar faces a tougher competitor than the German mark and the Japanese Yen for the top currency spot. Furthermore, the geopolitical global order has also changed. In the 1960s and 1980s, amid the Cold War, both Western Europe and Japan were dependent on the US military for their security. Today, the EU is lees threatened military; hence it has more room to act independently. More importantly, however, China is not a US military ally nor is it dependent on the US for its security, rather the opposite (Helleiner & Kirshner 2009). It is developing its own military arsenal and it has legitimate aspirations to be one, if not *the* hegemonic force in East Asia.

Thus, the balance of power in the IMS has changed. The US is not able to coerce or persuade as easily its trade partners to follow its directives. With the consolidation of the European Monetary Union (EMU), the Eurozone member states are now better protected (only to a certain extent, the current sovereign debt crisis has shown the limitations of this protection) from Dollar shocks and from US bullying in macroeconomic negotiations (Henning 1998; 2006). China, on its part, with $3 trillion in foreign reserves, is also able to resist better US pressure to revalue the Renminbi (Chin & Helleiner 2008). It is very unlikely that the Chinese leadership will accept a new Plaza Accord similar to the one conceded by Japan in 1985. As then, and in the early 1970s, the US needs a weaker Dollar to increase exports and rebalance its economy, and for that it wants China to de-peg substantially from the greenback. China, on the other hand, does not want to repeat the mistakes of Japan (Eichengreen 2011).

Instead of bowing to US pressure, it has maintained the peg and redoubled its efforts in blaming the US government for being the main cause of the global imbalances that led to the global financial crisis. In the view of Chinese policymakers the US structural current account deficits, consequence of the Triffin Dilemma, and the extreme loose monetary policy of the Federal Reserve (Quantitative Easing [QE] being just the most radical of such policies) are the most destabilising factors in the current Flexible-Dollar-Standard (FDS)[2] regime, based on free floating exchange rates and free capital flows. These policies have the intention to devalue the Dollar to deflect adjustment costs and as such can equally be classified as an act of currency manipulation. In this unstable scenario of 'currency wars', which can end up in trade protectionism, the positions of the main contenders seem to be opposed. While the US demands a floating Renminbi (RMB) in accordance with the prevalent 'rules' of the FDS,[3] China demands a

2 I use here the term Flexible-Dollar-Standard to differentiate it from the Dollar-Standard of the Bretton Woods period (1944–73) when the Dollar was linked to gold. By using this term, I distance myself from the view of other contributors in this issue that think that we are already in a multi-currency IMS. This might be the outcome in the medium to long term if the Dollar continues to loose ground but as of yet the Dollar still dominates double the share of the Euro (the second most used currency) in all the different functions of international money. Until this difference is narrowed, we are still in Dollar unipolarity, or in a One-and-a-Half (with the Euro the other half) system, as suggested by Cohen (2010).

3 'Rules' is here in quotes because since the collapse of Bretton Woods in the early 1970s, the IMS has increasingly followed the route reducing as many rules as possible. This started with the free floating of currencies and the free movement of capitals and continued with the progressive de-regulation of financial markets across the world (Helleiner 1994). This process, which found its legitimatisation upon the Efficient Market Hypothesis, was steered by the US in collaboration with the UK. As Blyth (2003) explains, both countries have favoured the free movement of capitals and the deregulation of financial markets in order to finance trough massive capital inflows their chronic and structural current account deficits. The efficiency of this increasingly deregulated IMS has been severely questioned in the wake of the global financial crisis, although it has to be said that this is just another financial crisis in the FDS. Since the collapse of Bretton Woods and the introduction of free flow of capitals there have been financial crises every few years (Stiglitz & Greenwald 2010). This is what Chinese policymakers want to avoid.

renegotiation of the status of the Dollar as the main international currency and the establishment of a more stable and coordinated international exchange rate regime less prone to recurrent financial crises (Chin & Wang 2010). Here China has gained certain allies lately. It counts with the explicit support of the other BRICS countries: Brazil, Russia, India and South Africa (*Xinhua* 2011), and also with several United Nations (UN) sponsored expert groups such as the Stiglitz Expert Commission (UN 2009) and UNCTAD (2009, 2010), which have all declared that the current system is unstable and hence a multilateral solution is urgently needed. Most surprisingly, a similar assessment has come recently from the IMF (2010), which until very recently did not dare to question the FDS.

Given this state of affairs, the role of the EU, and in particular of the Eurozone, has gained in importance. By issuing the second most used currency in the world,[4] the Eurozone holds considerable (latent) influence in the future management of the IMS. It is not only that the Eurozone is in a brokering position between the US, the largest debtor and declining hegemon, and China, the largest creditor and upcoming economic and political power, in the system. Most importantly, the Europeans have 50 years of experience in dealing with 'Dollar shocks' emanating from the inherent instabilities in the FDS (Marsh 2009; Jabko 2010). This provides them with considerable leverage when it comes to proposing multilateral solutions to overcome the structural problems inherent to the FDS. Chinese policymakers, for instance, are well aware that if they want to end Dollar hegemony and establish a more coordinated exchange rate regime

4 Latest data (March 2011) from the IMF COFER (Currency Composition of Official Foreign Exchange Reserves) show that the US Dollar counts for 61.4% of total share, while the Euro represents 26.3%. Latest data (December 2010) from the BIS Triennial Central Bank Survey on foreign exchange (FX) market activity show that the US Dollar's share is 84.9% (out of 200%, since there are always two currencies involved in every FX transaction) and that of the Euro is 39.1%. Finally, De La Dehesa (2009) shows that in international trade invoice the Euro represents 28.9% of invoice, while the Dollar accounts for 65%. As mentioned in the previous note, the Dollar still doubles the Euro in the role of store of value, medium of exchange and unit of account; therefore hitherto we are still in an IMS closer to unipolarity than to multi-polarity. The trend is towards multi-polarity, but we are not quite there yet.

they will need to count with European support and expertise in order to bring US policymakers to the negotiating table. But, the question is how much leverage do the Europeans actually have in reshaping the structure of the IMS in a more multilateral and coordinated fashion? And, most importantly, if they have this leverage, are they willing to use it? In other words, is their constant appeal for a more coordinated IMS (Barroso 2010) simple rhetoric or are they really working to achieve it? These are the two main questions that this chapter will address.

In order to find answers the next section will try to conceptualise how European and Chinese monetary power have advanced vis-à-vis US monetary power in the past decade. Building on Cohen's (2006a) monetary power concept, I will argue that the Europeans and the Chinese have gained greater monetary autonomy from the US. I will also claim that the Europeans have been able to exert certain influence in the third and second faces of power of preference-shaping and agenda-setting (Lukes 1974, 2005). Not least thanks to closer collaboration with the Chinese. However, the Eurozone is still unable and unwilling to make any significant impact in the first face of power where decisions are actually made. This theoretical analysis will then be supported empirically by presenting evidence collected through a review of the literature and near 30 in-depth, semi-structured elite interviews with policymakers and financial elites in China. The third section focuses upon the ideational effects that the Euro has generated among Chinese policymakers and the fourth section analysis the achievements and under-achievements of the Eurozone and China in the second and first faces of international monetary governance.

Conceptualising Europe's and China's monetary power

As the diagram shows (see Figure 1), when conceptualising monetary power I follow Strange's (1994, 1987) approach of combining four distinct but interlinked pillars in the generation of structural monetary power. These are the fields of security (military might), production (of goods and services), finance (creation of credit) and knowledge (including leadership in ideas). Without considerable influence in some or all of these different structures it is impossible for any country or union of countries to issue an international currency and gain monetary power. It is here to note that Strange's understanding of monetary power includes both material capabilities and ideational influences. In this regard, as Strange defined it:

> Structural power is the power to choose and to shape the structures of the global political economy within which other states, their political institutions, their economic enterprises, and (not least) their professional people have to operate. This means more than the power to set the agenda of discussion or to design the international 'regime' of rules and customs. (1987:565)

While Strange refers here to structural power in general, I argue that her overall structure is also applicable to the narrower concept of monetary power, as developed by Cohen (2006a). Whereas Cohen limits his analysis to the behavioural tradition[5] of focusing only on the first two faces of power (decision making and agenda-setting), as Strange suggests in her definition, it is also important to cover the more ideational third face of preference-shaping, as developed by Lukes (1974, 2005).

For Cohen (2006a) 'the macro-level dimension of monetary power consists, first and foremost, of a capacity to *avoid* payments adjustment costs, either by delaying adjustment or by deflecting the burden of adjustment on to others (2006a:31, italics in original). The best example in this case is the US.[6] To achieve that, Cohen argues that on a more general level the holder of international monetary power needs to develop autonomy and influence. *Autonomy* meaning that the agent is independent in its macroeconomic policies and *Influence* standing for the capacity of making others change their macroeconomic policies. Cohen is keen to highlight

5 For the two first faces of power, see Bachrach & Baratz (1962).

6 The US has been able, trough the centrality of the Dollar in the system, to run persistent current account deficits since the 1970s. In this regard it has been able to delay the adjustment process. Furthermore, whenever the adjustment process occurred, it was also able to deflect part of this adjustment upon its trading partners. Follow the discussion below.

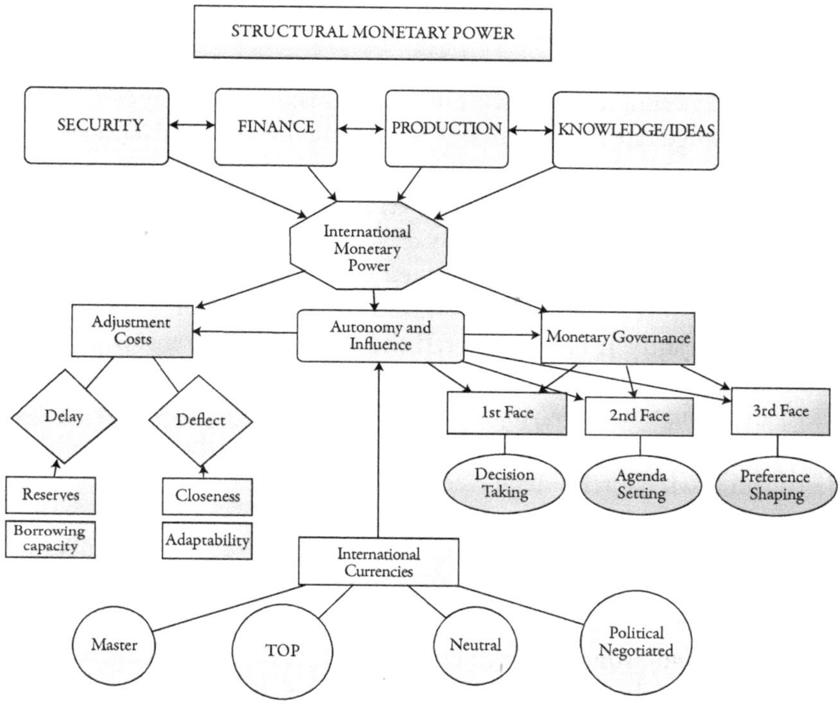

Figure 1: Diagram on Monetary Power.

that autonomy precedes influence. An agent can have autonomy, but this does not mean that she has influence.

This distinction is especially important when analysing Europe's monetary power. For Cohen (2008a), with the consolidation of the Euro, the Eurozone has enhanced its autonomy. Up to the recent sovereign debt crisis, which hit first Greece and then Ireland and Portugal, Eurozone peripheral member states were able to delay their adjustment processes, similarly to the US. Through the protection of EMU and the attractiveness of Euro denominated debt, countries such as Greece, Spain and Portugal were able to access cheaper credit than would otherwise be possible. It could be argued that this increased autonomy turned out to be detrimental because it encouraged a level of indebtedness that was unsustainable.

Nonetheless, this line of argument does not question the fact that these countries were able to live beyond their means and delay their adjustment.

Another example of how the Euro has increased autonomy can be seen in the exchange rate movements. With a currency able to absorb greater demand, the swings are less dramatic. Countries such as Germany, and even France (although to a lesser extent), were able to cope with a staggering 85% swing from the Euro's 2002 low of $0.86 to its all time high of $1.60 in 2008 without a total collapse of their export industries. Furthermore, it is not only that the Euro has reduced the swings against the Dollar. More importantly, it has eliminated the exchange rate tensions within EMU that were so common in previous crises, and an incentive to create EMU in the first place (Wyplosz 2009). As previously, it could be argued that the greater absorption and protection capacity of the Euro has been detrimental as it has reinforced Germany's export-led growth model, it has completely undermined the competitiveness of the rest of the Eurozone, who has carried most of the adjustment burden deflected by the US. While this is certainly an accurate analysis, again for this discussion it does not contest the notion that overall the Eurozone member states have been able to delay their adjustment processes. Rather, it points to the flaws that the Eurozone has at the governance and institutional level in dealing with its internal imbalances and its external representation in exchange rates. As explained by Savona (2010), 'the EU did not understand that the Euro needed a different external exchange rate regime –fixed or pegged, instead of floating– to protect itself from the conversion of the Dollar-denominated official reserves of other countries into Euros', chief among them China. In other words, one can say that the Euro was the victim of its own success. By gaining autonomy, the Eurozone periphery was able to delay adjustment and absorb more of the adjustment costs deflected by the US. But at some point this absorption capacity reached its limit and exposed the internal contradictions in EMU (Vermeiren 2011).

Finally, EMU has given the Eurozone member states also more protection against US influence in macroeconomic diplomatic negotiations. As Henning (1998, 2006) has demonstrated, before the consolidation of EMU the small and medium sized economies of the EU were vulnerable to US macroeconomic bullying (including the threat of withdrawing the security umbrella)[7] because they had to deal with the big power individually. This has changed slightly with the Euro. Once the Europeans agree on one position, it is more difficult for the Americans to convince them to change their behaviour. A good example of this is the recent spat at the G20 between the US and the Europeans in relation to continuing with expansionary policies, as advocated by the Obama administration, or starting with consolidation programmes, as defended by the Europeans as a bloc (Beattie & Peel 2010).

More resilience to US macroeconomic diplomatic pressure is also to be seen in China's behaviour. For almost a decade, US policymakers have tried to persuade their Chinese counterparts to de-peg from the Dollar and revalue substantially the RMB. With the mammoth sum of $3 trillion[8] in foreign reserves, however, the Chinese have been able to resist this pressure. With this high amount of reserves, roughly 65% of them denominated in US Dollars (*Reuters* 2010), China has acquired greater protection and therefore higher autonomy.[9] It has enough reserves to withstand any speculative attack coming from financial institutions operating out of Wall Street, and in the last case scenario it can also threaten the US with dumping its Dollars, and hence provoke a collapse in the value of its

7 As Henning (1998) highlights, the US achieved in numerous occasions in the 1960s and 1970s (in the midst of the Cold War) an appreciation of the Deutsche Mark by threatening Germany with withdrawing its troops. The security card played also an important role in the 1980s when Japan agreed to appreciate the Yen in the 1985 Plaza Accord (Kirshner 2009). This is why it is important to consider the security aspect when conceptualising monetary power (see diagram in Figure 1).

8 Figure provided by the People's Bank of China as of the end of March 2011.

9 Scholars such as Krugman (2009) have argued that China's bloating foreign reserves are an indication of weakness, not strength. Arguing that China is in a 'Dollar trap', Krugman criticises the Chinese government for maintaining its currency undervalued and not undertake the structural reforms that would be triggered by a RMB appreciation. The view is certainly different from Beijing. From this perspective, accumulation of reserves in Dollars is a product of the loose monetary policy of the FED. The Chinese government needs to sterilise all this unwanted liquidity in order to avoid damaging imported inflation. Essentially, by accumulating US debt, China just recycles the Dollars printed by the US (Chin & Helleiner 2008).

currency. The foreign reserves function thus as a financial 'nuclear' deterrence mechanism which allows China to decide when and at what pace to start its adjustment process from an export-led to a domestic consumption-led growth model. The US is trying through 'currency war' mechanisms (i.e. Quantitative Easing) to devalue the Dollar and appreciate the RMB, but China is eager and capable to resist (Zhang Monan 2010). As Chin and Helleiner (2008) acknowledge, by maintaining capital controls and a heavily regulated banking system, China is better suited to sterilise the constant new entrance of Dollar inflows than Germany and Japan where in the 1970s and 1980s, respectively.

Nevertheless, autonomy does not mean that the Europeans and the Chinese have automatically acquired what Cohen describes as *active* influence. Cohen argues that the Europeans lack the latter because they are still politically divided (which they are) and in consequence they are not able to project their newly gained monetary power in the governance of the IMS. Hence, Cohen believes that 'the Europeans clearly are now better placed to resist external pressures. Their collective autonomy has been enhanced. But Europe is still a long way from exercising the kind of leverage that monetary union might have been expected to give it. Influence has not been effectively actualized' (2008a:460), especially when it comes to avoid excessive exchange rates movements. As for China, Cohen recognises that with the accumulation of huge reserves China has developed a nuclear capability in financial matters, especially against the US. However, this threat is difficult to utilise. 'Any depreciation of the greenback would impose costs on China as well, in form of capital losses on remaining holdings'. Therefore, one can say that 'global imbalances too have caused a shift in the balance of monetary power – but, as in the case of EMU, mainly in the dimension of autonomy' (Cohen 2008a:462).

While Cohen's analysis is accurate in identifying the policy outcomes, it does not cover all the different layers of monetary power. To do so, I argue that his conceptual mapping needs to be expanded. Strange's framework consistent of four interlinked and interdependent sides (Security, Finance, Production and Knowledge and Ideas, see Figure 1) provides a far more holistic understanding of how monetary power is to be gained. Both in finance and production, for instance, the EU and China have gained more ground versus the US than Cohen acknowledges. The Eurozone, for instance, has been making progress in the integration of its financial markets (Galati & Wooldridge 2006; De la Dehesa 2009). China on its part has started a 'Going Global' strategy increasing substantially its foreign direct investment, its foreign aid and promoting its currency for international trade (Chin & Helleiner 2008; Cookson & Dyer 2010; Dyer et al. 2011). Furthermore, when it comes to production, in the 2010 Forbes list of Top 100 companies, the Eurozone has actually the same number of companies (27) than the US, showing that the global production capacity of both economies is very similar. The Euro would not have been able to become the second most used international currency without the global reach of European companies.

The great difference though lies in the security side. That the Eurozone is still dependent on the US for its security is certainly an important factor in explaining why the Eurozone has not developed further its monetary influence. Military might is an important factor in generating monetary power. As Helleiner and Kirshner (2009) explain, the centrality of the Dollar in the IMS is not only due to the fact that it is the *top* international currency of the top economy in the world. In some instances the Dollar's centrality can be explained better through the concept of *negotiated* currency (see again Figure 1) since key countries such as Saudi Arabia and Japan use it partly (or predominantly) in their international transactions because the US provides them with military security.[10] China might at some point challenge the US in this field, but thus far the threat is minimal. As

10 The taxonomy of master, top, neutral and negotiated international currencies comes from Susan Strange (1971). Following this classification, the Euro is today a *neutral* international currency. It functions as a good diversification tool in investment portfolios, but the European authorities have no aspirations to make it the *top* international currency. Strange's taxonomy is important to understand the link between international currencies and political power and economic power. To issue a master or negotiated international currency, the issuer needs political-military power. To issue a neutral one it doesn't. History shows that normally the issuer of the top currency is at the same time the major economy and military power.

for Europe, its military dependence to the US makes it cautious in relation to propose any changes in the IMS that might go against US interests.

Having referred here to the military might of the US, it would be disingenuous to claim that Cohen does not take military power into account when discussing monetary matters. He might not refer to it explicitly when he explains monetary power, but he has certainly included military issues when discussing the Dollar vs. Euro rivalry (2006b; 2009). Thus, his wider approach on monetary power includes both relational power based on military capabilities and diplomatic statecraft, but also certain notions of Strange's structural power, especially when it comes to finance. Cohen covers then what is commonly understood in the literature as the two first faces of power. The first face focusing on government-to-government decision-making negotiations and the second centred around market induced structural conditions which ultimately determine, to a certain extent, the agenda of these negotiations and the policies derived from them. However, where Cohen falls short, as he himself admits (2006a:34), is in covering what is known as the third face of power emerging from the realm of ideas. This third face of power has been highlighted by Lukes by arguing that '*A* may exercise power over *B* getting him to do what he does not want to do, but he also exercises power over him by *influencing, shaping or determining* his very wants' (1974:23, emphasis added). This influence is realised through certain structures, institutions and norms, but also through discourses and ideas. While Lukes refers to this third face in terms of what could be described as propaganda by the ruling capitalist classes, I use the third face of power not only in this coercive, top-down approach.[11] Rather, I understand the third face of preference-shaping as the realm where the battle of ideas takes place. These ideas might be those of the hegemonic

11 It is to note here that in his 1974 conception of power, Lukes referred to this third dimension by only considering aspects related to domination. In 2005, however, he recognises that 'it was a mistake to define power by saying that "A exercises power over B when A affects B in a manner contrary to B's interests"' (Lukes 2005:12). Lukes proceeds by saying that 'power is a capacity not the exercise of that capacity [...] you can be powerful by satisfying and advancing other's interests' (Lukes 2005:12). It is this type of power that I apply here.

country in monetary affairs, supported by its relational (military) power and the other three sides of Strange's structural power, but they might also be the ideas of countries and agents that want to reshape the IMS in their favour. Hence, I conceive ideas as both necessary tools to perpetuate the established monetary order (the idea that free floating of exchange rates and capital movements make the system efficient is a case in point) but equally as enabling factors to change the status quo, especially in times of crisis and uncertainty as is presently the case. As Blyth suggests, 'ideas allow agents to reduce uncertainty, propose a particular solution to a moment of crisis, and empower agents to resolve that crisis by constructing new institutions in line with these new ideas' (2002:11).

As will be demonstrated in the next session, I argue that the Euro symbolises a move away from the instabilities of the FDS. The creation and consolidation of EMU has had three layers of ideational effects in the minds of Chinese financial elites. First, it has shown them that regional monetary cooperation is a good protection mechanism against the financial volatilities associated to the FDS. If there is a project in the world that has moved away completely from destabilising exchange rate movements among trading partners, this is the Eurozone. EMU is hence seen as a possible template for regional monetary cooperation and even monetary union in East Asia. Second, given that EMU is still a harbinger in relation to regional monetary cooperation (it has been partly successful so far, but its long term feasibility is not assured), Chinese policymakers are looking at how the Euro has been able to become an international currency in less than a decade and they would like to emulate this (so far) successful trajectory with the RMB, especially when it comes to invoicing trade. The rise of the Euro has taught them that an IMS with several international currencies is possible, and perhaps even desirable. With the coming of the Euro, the common sense perception that the most efficient IMS is one where only one currency is dominant (Kindleberger 1986; 2000) is put into question. Third, the success so far of the Euro has shown that peaceful and voluntary sovereignty-sharing in monetary affairs is feasible. Something that before was seen as impossible, is now perceived as a possibility, not only at the regional level, but even at the global level. The utopia of establishing one day a global currency as Keynes suggested with his Bancor idea remains a dream, but the *idea* of the Euro brings this dream closer. The creation of a supranational global currency might be very difficult to achieve. Recent tensions within the Eurozone show how difficult it is to have a monetary union, without a fiscal and political union to buffer the adjustments that would otherwise be smoothen out by exchange rate movements. But one does not need to go thus far to acknowledge the ideational effects of the Euro. The more mundane goal to achieve monetary cooperation at a global level to avoid the problems associated to the Triffin Dilemma, and destabilising exchange rates, seems to be sufficient progress in the right direction for Chinese policymakers (Zhou 2009, 2011; Chin & Wang 2010). Thus, the European experience in multilateral negotiations is a good know-how basis upon which to move this process forward. In this regard, although still far from its potential, European monetary influence might be greater than widely acknowledged.

The ideational impact of the Euro in the third face of power

Due to space restrictions, it is impossible here to present substantial evidence to support the argument that the Euro is performing a template role in the promotion of regional monetary cooperation or even monetary unions around the world. A good summary of this evidence can be found somewhere else (Otero-Iglesias 2011). It suffices here to say that the role model potential of the Euro has been mentioned by other authors. Marsh (2009) for example acknowledges that 'in Asia, Latin America and the Middle East, the Euro supplies a template for a wide range of regional monetary unions that may be established in coming years' (2009:2). Even Cohen engages with this same idea by stating that 'EMU is clearly viewed as a test case for a strategy of pooling, rather than surrendering, monetary sovereignty. If Europe's experiment comes to be seen as a success, it could have a powerful demonstration effect, encouraging similar initiatives elsewhere' (2008b:231). The role model effects of the Euro in East Asia have also been covered in detail by Eichengreen (2007), although he is sceptical about the prospects of an East Asian monetary union.

However, my research findings show that these symbolic effects of the Euro are not only reduced to the regional level. They are also influencing how key policymakers and financial elites in emerging markets, including China, socially construct the evolution of the IMS. As was explained in the theoretical section, the Euro has had three main ideational effects. The first relates to regional monetary cooperation. The second has to do with the increased perception that with the consolidation of the Euro we are increasingly entering in a transition phase from Dollar unipolarity to a multi-currency system, where not only the Euro but also other currencies, especially the RMB, compete with the Dollar. Since 2009, against the backdrop of the global financial crisis, China has started a multi-phase campaign to increase the use of the RMB in international trade (Cookson & Dyer 2010; Subacchi 2010; Eichengreen 2011), and as one Chinese official disclosed, the lessons drawn from the internationalisation process of the Euro provide a good template on how to develop this strategy successfully (Interview X-3 2009). Again, unfortunately there is not enough space here to elaborate further on this ideational trend. However, it suffices here to reproduce the words of Qin Yaqing, senior member of the Foreign Policy Advisory Group of the Ministry of Foreign Affairs of China, who provides a good summary of the general feeling about the future of the IMS.

> The global financial crisis has shown the institutional deficiencies of the Dollar system. Only one currency can bring stability but also instability. I am of the belief that a few currencies can bring more stability to the system. This is what I would call the benefits of 'benign competition' ... I believe that in the future we will have three major international currencies: the Dollar, the Euro and a currency from Asia (either the RMB or an Asian currency). [...] With this currency triangle the global institutions have the potential to get stronger, to begin delivering again.[12] (Qin 2009)

The Euro has provoked also some mind changes – and this is its third effect – on the possibility of establishing multilateral cooperation in an increasingly multi-currency system. For a number of interviewees, Zhou

12 Single quotes are used here to signify that I paraphrase the source. Most interviews in China were not recorded, therefore I write the statements out of my own notes and not from the recording.

Xiaochuan's (2009) proposal in favour of SDRs is based on the success of EMU. Ding Yifan, director of the Development and Research Centre, a think tank directly funded by the State Council, the Chinese cabinet, explains neatly this argument. He says that the Euro is an example to follow. 'Zhou Xiaochuan's proposal of a supranational currency has the Euro as reference. If you can achieve regional monetary integration, then you can also achieve world monetary integration. The Euro is a role model. If the Euro succeeds, then the idea of a world currency will get even stronger' (Ding 2009). Further evidential triangulation supports this argument. Another researcher at the Chinese Academy of Social Sciences (CASS), a think tank close to the Chinese government, who asked to remain anonymous (Interview X-25, 2009), confirmed that for several years an Italian central banker (whose name cannot be disclosed) would constantly speak about SDRs with researchers at CASS and that more recently he had entered in contact with the Chinese central bank to explain the proposal. For Jamil Anderlini, correspondent of the *Financial Times* in Beijing, the connection makes perfectly sense. 'The Euro is the only super-sovereign currency that is around, so I guess this must have had some influence on Zhou' (Anderlini 2009). There is also evidence that Robert Mundell is advising China on the reform of the IMS (Webb 2008), and as is widely known Mundell was also influential in the creation of the Euro. Mundell (2005) is also a great advocate for a more managed exchange rate regime and eventually for the creation of a global currency.

Overall, the sense is that before the existence of the Euro *the idea* of sharing willingly and peacefully monetary sovereignty was a desirable but unfeasible objective, while with the consolidation of EMU this utopia might be less impossible. Thus, the hitherto success of the Euro has given the Europeans a considerable degree of respect. In the ideational third face of preference-shaping they count with certain influence due to their perceived expertise and know-how in monetary multilateralism. This has encouraged policymakers in China to ask the Europeans to go beyond the realm of the third face and, on the basis of their regional success in dealing with the instabilities of the FDS, start actively cooperating with China in the reform of the IMS. The feeling is that 'Europe should join in the efforts to create a more balanced and fair economic system ... [Since] excessive dependence on the US Dollar makes all of us very vulnerable [...] If Europe and emerging economies cooperate on the issue [of promoting the use of SDRs], it will at least put pressure on the US to be more prudent with its monetary policy. We can put the issue on the agenda, rather than leaving it up in the air' (Wang 2009, brackets added). In general, 'the consensus Chinese view is that a multi-reserve currency era is coming, even if only gradually, and that it would be in China's strategic interests to promote such a scenario' (Chin & Wang 2010). For that China needs to find alliances and the best partner would be the EU. As Chin and Helleiner (2008) explain China has certainly acquired a higher degree of monetary autonomy with its immense foreign reserves. As the main creditor nation of the world, surpassing even the World Bank in international aid in 2010 (Dyer et al. 2010), China has been able to exercise more influence and political leverage than Cohen (2008a) acknowledges. However, similarly to Europe, China has not been able to convert this increased influence in changing the rules of the IMS game. This is partly because China has followed Deng Xiaoping's advice of keeping a low profile in international negotiations, but also partly because the debate in China on how to establish an alternative IMS is still in its infant stages (Chin & Wang 2010). This is why China has been looking to Europe to help it to bring the reform of the IMS on to the G20 agenda. Some Chinese officials interviewed in March 2009 would especially count with French collaboration in this regard, since in their opinion the French have always been very keen in moving away from the FDS (Interview X-18 2009).

At first one must say that the Europeans responded lukewarmly to Chinese calls for the end of the FDS. When Zhou Xiaochuan (2009) published his article on the reform of the IMS, the response from Europe was muted. During that time one official from the European Commission (EC) office in Beijing would state that the official guideline coming from Brussels about Zhou's proposal was to say that 'Europe takes note of the proposal, but nothing more' (Interview X-10 2009). As of that point, it seemed that the Europeans were happy to leave their monetary power restrained to the third face of power. The view among the Europeans was that it would be unwise to side with China and the BRICS on this highly sensitive issue because it could alienate the Americans. Nonetheless, in April 2010 when asked about Europe's muteness on this topic, EC president Barroso replied that it was not true that Europe did not have a position on this issue and that it was not working on it. His response was that 'Europe has consistently called for *more coordination in the exchange rates of the major currencies*. Europe has also always said that the IMS should not be dominated by one single currency, such as the Dollar, but be formed by several international currencies, being the Euro one of them'. He did also say that 'the European Troika (consisting of the head of the Eurozone, the commissioner of Monetary and Economic Affairs and the president of the ECB) was working with all the trading partners on this issue and that this topic was high on the agenda' (Barroso 2010). Further evidential triangulation confirms this statement. It appears that the members of the European Troika and their Chinese counterparts have been meeting since November 2007, under the umbrella of what is now called the EU-China High Level Economic and Trade Dialogue (HED), with the objective to 'take comprehensive measures to step up economic structural adjustments and *prevent big fluctuations in the foreign exchange rates*, while at the same time make a contribution to the orderly adjustment of global imbalances' (*Xinhua* 2007, emphasis added).

However, despite these diplomatic encounters, up to 2010 Europe's role in the reform of the IMS was certainly disappointing from the point of view of the financial elites of China. The EU's mantra about seeking further coordination in the exchange rate regime was more seen as a cover up for siding with the US in demanding an appreciation of the RMB (Waldmeir 2009). Europe's subordination to the US, which opposes any move out of flexible exchange rates and the centrality of the Dollar in the system, is something that is continuously criticised by Chinese policymakers. The vast majority of participants interviewed would like to see a more independent and assertive Europe that can act as a counter-balance to the US. The same demand comes also from European figures such as Jacques Delors, former EC president, who states that 'it is time that the leaders of EMU live up to their responsibility, not to see the Euro substituting the Dollar, but rather in contributing to create a more balanced monetary system' (Vidal-Folch 2009). A similar complaint comes also from Cao Honghui, director of the Financial Markets Division of the Institute of Finance and Banking at CASS. He does also want the Europeans to be more proactive in reforming the governance structures of IMS. 'The IMF is totally controlled by the US', he argues, 'they have veto power because of the voting system, but even leaving the voting system aside, the truth is that the IMF is completely controlled by the US. We do not trust the IMF at all. As for the Europeans, yes, they appoint the general director, but this is only to save their face. They need to do more' (Cao 2009).

The French push to enhance EMU's monetary power in the second face

Even though the Europeans as a united bloc have not come out with a clear position on China's calls for the reform of the IMS, the French government has had a different approach. In July 2009 at the G8–G5 meeting in Italy, President Sarkozy supported Chinese attempts to reform the FDS by saying that 'we cannot stick with one single currency ... we've still got the Bretton Woods system of 1945 ... 60 years afterwards we've got to ask: shouldn't a politically multipolar world correspond to an economically multi-currency world?' (Thomas 2009). Six months later at the economic forum in Davos the French president announced that 'we need a new Bretton Woods. We cannot preach free trade and tolerate monetary dumping [in a clear allusion to what later would be called Currency Wars]. France, which will chair G20 in 2011, will place reform of the monetary system on the agenda' (Tett & Hall 2010, brackets added). After seeing how Chinese calls for reform were hardly addressed during the 2009 G20 presidency held by the United Kingdom, a country that has never hidden its reluctance to change the status quo, the French seemed to be determined to push the reform of the IMS on to the G20 agenda. For this they knew that they could count with Chinese support.

Both France and China have always favoured the implementation of 'mechanisms for *avoiding excessive exchange rate volatility*' (emphasis added), they have persistently called for a 'debate on the international doctrine of capital movements' and they have always sought to 'curb commodity speculation', precisely the three main themes that Sarkozy put on the table when he proposed for the first time the French G20 agenda in August 2010. In this same presentation there was also a hint that France and China were working together on the formulation of this agenda. Sarkozy made clear that there is the need for a 'new framework for consultation of exchange rate developments' and that China should join the G7 meetings of finance ministers in this area (Hall 2010, all quotes in this paragraph). Here we see how France would be very willing to welcome China on board because in the current configuration of the G7 its influence is curtailed. The US, the UK, Canada and Germany are all countries which are sceptical about state dirigisme in the foreign exchange markets, Japan is more inclined to do so, but it has not the diplomatic clout to challenge the US on this issue. This leaves only Italy as a potential ally to France. With the entry of China in the G7, however, the balance of power would be very different.

Given that France and China prefer a more managed and multi-polar exchange rate regime than the FDS, it is no wonder then to discover that diplomatic cooperation has been close in recent times. French and Chinese officials have been meeting for some time to design strategies to reform the IMS. Interestingly, 'the talks and their content have been kept secret, in an attempt to draw China into a discussion on global currency coordination' (Hollinger & Giles 2010). Again here the important issue is to define what the Europeans mean by 'currency coordination'. If this means that the Chinese need to float their currency, then the conversation ends right there. China is firmly opposed to completely flexible exchange rates determined only by market forces. This is perceived to be too unstable. The boat cannot be left to its own mercy against the waves of possible storms. It needs to be steered by the 'public hand'. As a senior official disclosed, the Chinese proposal to avoid international exchange rates disruptions is as follows: 'the US, EMU, Japan and the UK should agree to a managed-floating exchange rate band. The Chinese RMB would remain more or less pegged to the Dollar. This would hold until China develops its financial markets. Once this is achieved, the RMB will start gradually its floating process, join the other strong currencies in the established band and consequently be part of the IMF SDRs basket, which hopefully will become the future reserve currency' (Interview X-3 2009). From the onset this proposal would certainly find the favour of the French who have always advocated a managed exchange rate regime. It is very doubtful, though, whether the US, the UK and Germany would accept this proposal.

What is by now confirmed is that the French have been able to impose their agenda on the workings of the G20 for 2011. The reform of the IMS is now the most important topic discussed in the G20 and the IMF. This proves that the Europeans have enough structural power (in the realms of production, finance and ideas) to leverage certain influence in the second face of power focused on the ability to shape the agenda. While for many commentators, especially for US experts, 'Sarkozy's campaign is mainly political theatre' to win points in the run up to the 2012 presidential election in France (Beattie 2011), it would be disingenuous to overlook the achievements of French diplomacy. Right after the G20 meeting in Seoul in November 2010, Sarkozy (2010) was keen to highlight these achievements. He confirmed that France, despite considerable opposition (presumably from the US), had been able to make the reform of the IMS as the most important point in the G20 agenda. France has also convinced China to hold a high level conference on the reform of the IMS. That China has agreed to this is already an achievement. As the same Sarkozy would recognise, 'it was already not that easy – to be absolutely frank – to get the organization of a seminar on the international monetary system in China' (Sarkozy 2010). In spring 2009 when I did my fieldwork in Beijing, a number of participants would state that China did not want to take the responsibility of hosting any G20 gathering because it did not have the capacity, expertise or the diplomatic clout to organise such an event. Thanks to French persuasion, this seems to have changed. Interestingly, the Nanjing meeting in March 2011 showed clearly the opposing positions of the different players. While France is in favour of including China in the G7 and the RMB in the SDR basket, the US has made clear that it will not accept this proposal until China lets the RMB float freely, establishes an independent central bank and lifts its capital controls. Needless to say that China will not accept these conditions in the foreseeable future (Anderlini 2011).[13]

13 During this seminar an unnamed senior German official disclosed for the first time that 'Berlin was also in favour of currency questions being addressed by a broader

Notwithstanding, these opposing views, the French zeal to initiate the debate (and thus spread ideas) on the future reconfiguration of the IMS has produced already a number of reports at the multilateral level. It is worthwhile highlighting here the Palais-Royal Initiative (PRI), which was set up to: 1) Come to a multilateral consensual assessment on the current problems of the IMS; and 2) Propose concrete solutions to tackle these problems. It is interesting to see how the French focus is to arrive to a common narrative on the problems of the FDS. As Blyth (2002) explains, in every systemic reform of the world economy, the first battle of ideas lies in winning the argument on what is wrong with the current system and why it needs to be reformed. Once this is achieved, the next step is then to come up with ideas on how to reform it. The PRI has been led by Camdessus, Lamfalussy and the very recently defunct Padoa-Schioppa, all high-profile former European officials in monetary affairs. It includes also Truman and Volcker, two former US policymakers, and a wide range of former and current officials from emerging markets, including Hu Xiaolan, currently the vice president of China Society of Finance and Banking. These experts have identified several flaws in the FDS: the lack of mechanisms to deal with global imbalances; the financial excesses in certain countries and the creation of destabilising capital flows (in a clear criticism to US monetary policy); excessive exchange rate fluctuations deviated from fundamentals and driven my speculation (a factor consistently highlighted by China, see Zhou [2011]); and finally the excessive accumulation of reserves and how the diversification of these out of the Dollar can provoke financial havoc (in clear reference to China's conundrum in relation to its huge Dollar holdings). The solutions proposed thus far are: to increase the multilateral mechanisms of adjustment and surveillance; to adopt benchmarks based on macroeconomic fundamentals in order to avoid instability and misalignment in the exchange rates; to consider the adoption of capital controls when incoming flows are too destabilising (something that until very recently was considered heresy) and, finally, to promote the use of

---

group than the G7, perhaps incorporating the four BRIC countries – Brazil, Russia, India, China – along with Mexico (see Flynn & Yao 2011).

the SDRs as an alternative multilateral reserve currency (PRI 2011). These proposals are currently debated within the G20 framework.

As a matter of fact, after recent pressure from France and China, the promotion of SDRs is now again a topic that not only attracts the interest of academics (Julius 2010, Kenen 2010, Bergsten 2009) and UN agencies (Stiglitz Commission [UN 2009]; UNCTAD 2009); it is an issue that has been debated also by the executive board of the IMF after receiving several technical reports (Cooper 2011; IMF 2011a). While acknowledging the technical and political challenges that SDR promotion faces, the directors of the board agreed to consider 'ways to encourage the development of the SDR as a unit of account for private and official transactions, particularly the potential for developing a market for SDR-denominated assets' (IMF 2011b), certainly a prerequisite if the SDRs wants to have any chance to be globally appealing (Eichengreen 2011).

Whether these efforts to reform the current FDS bring some tangible results is to be seen. There are many analysts sceptical about any substantial overhaul of the current system (Beattie 2011; Eichengreen 2011) given that the US, still the most powerful country, with more structural power than any other, sticks to its beliefs that it has more to lose than to win from these reforms. The exorbitant privilege is not something that any country is willing to give up easily. Recent events have just shown how advantageous such a privilege is. While Europe, lacking a fiscal union to support its monetary union, needs to go now through painful austerity processes of adjustment, the US has been able to overcome one of the fiercest recessions in its history with an unprecedented loose fiscal and monetary policy. While the Europeans, especially the Germans, and the Chinese want the US to adjust through deflation, similarly to the Eurozone periphery, the US is unlikely to accept the same destiny. Rather, it will inflate its way out of its debt and so continue to deflect some of the adjustment costs upon others. As Wolf explains, in the current scenario of currency wars, 'the US wants to inflate the rest of the world, while the latter is trying to deflate the US. The US must win, since it has infinite ammunition: there is no limit to the Dollars the Federal Reserve can create' (Wolf 2010).

So, while the Europeans, through EMU, have gained autonomy and leveraged certain influence up to the second face of power in the form of spreading ideas about possible alternatives to the FDS and shaping the agenda to reform it, they are still a long way to make any significant impact in the first face where the rules of the game of the IMS are actually decided. The main reason for that is that they do not have the political unity to go beyond the second face. Sarkozy (2010) has stated that he counts with Germany in its reform efforts, especially now that Germany has agreed to co-chair, alongside Mexico, the G20 working group on the reform of the IMS. But until the Europeans speak with one united voice at the global stage their position will be too weak to impose any substantial change to the status quo, as has been acknowledged before by Bini-Smaghi (2006), executive director at the ECB. As stated above, it is doubtful whether Germany would back French and Chinese attempts to establish a more managed exchange rate regime since the current status quo of an overvalued Euro seems to work to its favour. The US deflection strategy of letting the Dollar fall to regain competitiveness, which can be traced back to the year 2002 (McKinnon 2010), has hurt especially Germany's main European exporting rivals: Italy and France, who have struggled with a Euro above $1.30, but for German companies an overvalued Euro has been less harmful. This intra-European competition is certainly a handicap in constructing a united European monetary diplomacy able to counterbalance US monetary power. This is rather unfortunate, since as Robert Mundell has argued, 'the swings in the Dollar-Euro exchange rate are big problems, and the problem is exacerbated by the fact that the Americans get the benefit of the swings and Europe gets the wrong end of the stick' (Webb 2008). The Eurozone sovereign debt crisis is partly consequence of the persistent overvaluation of the Euro, which undermines the competitiveness of the Eurozone periphery.

Conclusion

The main objective of this chapter has been to discern where the Eurozone stands within the framework of increased 'currency wars' and whether it is able and willing to change the current unregulated IMS, based on the flexible-Dollar-standard (FDS), to a more coordinated and managed exchange rate regime. The answer is that the Eurozone has made certain progress in the latter two faces of monetary power but as yet not in the first. France has certainly made some efforts, with the support of China, to start the debate on the transformation of the FDS. On the back of the ideational impact of EMU and the internationalisation process of the Euro, the French have gained enough leverage to make considerable impact in the second and third faces of power focused on preference-shaping and agenda-setting. However, by not being united, the Europeans preclude any possibility to force the US to enter into a compromise and relinquish the exorbitant privilege that the centrality of the Dollar offers them. Britain is unlikely to challenge its closest ally, and Germany has traditionally tried to avoid being too confrontational with the US. It is also doubtful whether Germany is totally committed to changing the status quo. The past decade has shown that it can live with an overvalued Euro much better than its European partners. Therefore, it is not only that the Europeans have not enough clout to change the IMS. Even if they were to have it, it is doubtful whether they would use it. Nonetheless, one cannot underestimate the impact that EMU has had in the reconfiguration of the IMS. The Euro has shown that regional monetary integration is possible, that a system with a number of international currencies might be more stable than dysfunctional Dollar unipolarity, and that multilateral cooperation in governing the IMS can draw lessons from the European experience. Other authors such as Calleo (2009) have already pointed to 'Europe's pluralist model' as a role model for a more integrated global monetary system without US hegemony. The drawback of the role model appeal of EMU is that it is still an experiment in the making. The recent sovereign debt crisis has shown its structural flaws. As of the time of writing the Eurozone is at a crossroads. Either it ingrates further towards a fiscal union, or it gives up the experiment and it returns to national currencies. In this debate I would side with Eichengreen (2011), who believes that the Euro will come out of this crisis stronger.

Thus, if we go back to Susan Strange's four sides of structural power, the Euro is carving out some of the foundations. Militarily the US is still dominant (here only China can change this in the long term). On the production side, the US and the Eurozone are on a very similar level, and if one takes the EU as a whole, the Europeans might be actually more dominant (in this area the BRICs, especially China, are catching up fast). In finance, however, the US remains by far the leading force. US financial power is proven by the centrality of Wall Street and the Dollar in the IMS. Nonetheless, it is also true that there has been a gradual diversification movement out of the greenback. The large current account deficits of the US, consequence of the Triffin Dilemma, are starting to unsettle international investors, including China. The Dollar is slowly losing its anchor and leading role and becoming increasingly a negotiable currency. As Zhang Ming (2009), a leading Chinese scholar on the reform of the IMS suggests, there are three potential adjustment routes to reduce the global imbalances of the FDS. The first one is what he calls a market driven solution whereby countries like China shift great amounts of their foreign reserve portfolios out of the Dollar before it collapses. It is here worth highlighting that what he sees as a 'market led adjustment' is seen in the West as the 'nuclear option'. The second possibility is that surplus countries appreciate their currencies under US unilateral pressure (the US is attempting to apply this deflection mechanism, but hitherto it is only working with the Eurozone and not with China). Finally, the third option would be to find cooperative cost-sharing mechanisms to smoothen the adjustment costs. In his opinion the consolidation of the SDRs (with the inclusion of the RMB in the basket) as the super-sovereign reserve currency in global trade and investment activity could be the right consensual solution to this conundrum. It would eliminate the Triffin Dilemma at its root and it would create a competition mechanism for the issuing authorities of the main currencies which would force them to restrain their monetary policy excesses.

In this sense, the ideational appeal of the Euro (if it survives) is undeniable. As mentioned, if monetary cooperation is possible at the regional level, theoretically it can also be achieved at the global level. The big question is whether the US will be ready to enter into a compromise. Up to very recently, US officials have consistently rejected any attempt to overhaul the FDS through multilateral negotiations, but perhaps things are starting to change. US treasury secretary Geithner's recent proposal to establish a 4%

to GDP benchmark for deficit and surplus countries seems a change in policy. For the first time the US advocates the 'public hand' in managing the global economy. FED chair, Bernanke (2010), did also surprise analysts when he stated recently that as 'currently constituted, the IMS has a structural flaw: It lacks a mechanism, market based, or otherwise, to induce needed adjustments by surplus countries, which can result in persistent imbalances'. Of course, with these words he continues to point the finger towards China for not revaluing, but that the head of the FED recognises that the FDS is structurally flawed is per se a change in attitude. The US might start to realise that it is in its best interest to find a multilateral solution to the current problems of the FDS. As Stiglitz (2009) has warned, 'whether the US likes it or not, the Dollar reserve system is fraying; the question is only whether we move from the current system to an alternative in haphazard way or in a more careful and structured way'. In this regard, it is important to follow closely in the next years the possible partnership of the Eurozone and China in reforming the IMS. While until the recent crisis the Europeans (with the exception of the French) were siding with the US in maintaining the status quo, now they are starting to be more vocal in their criticisms. The German finance minister, Schäuble has dared to call the current extra-loose US monetary policy 'clueless' (Breidthardt & Rohan 2010). The current sovereign debt crisis in the Eurozone has also strengthened the ties between the Europeans and China. There are not few investors, among them George Soros, who believe that the Chinese have actually saved the Euro in a critical moment (White 2010, see chapter 4 in this volume.). While Anglo-American hedge funds have been betting against the Euro, China has used the opportunity to increase its purchases of European debt and its investments in the Eurozone (Mallet & Wiesmann 2011). With this strategy it does not only want to diversify further from Dollar-denominated assets, it does also want to win political leverage in order to have the Eurozone as a strategic partner in the reconfiguration of the IMS. For the Chinese, the Europeans are seen as the brokers between the US, the current weakening hegemon, and China, the upcoming emerging power. And, as in every deal, it is always good to have the broker on your side. Another different question is whether the Eurozone can effectively perform the role of deal-breaker. So far, it is not.

References

Anderlini, J. (2009) Interview with author, St. Regis Hotel, Beijing, 6 April 2009.

Anderlini, J. (2011) 'Sarkozy urges G20 to hasten monetary reform', *Financial Times*, 31 March 2011.

Barroso, J. M. (2010) Keynote Speech (and Q&A session) to the Garnet Conference: *The European Union in International Affairs II*, Paleis der Academiën, Brussels, 22 April 2010.

Beattie, A. (2011) 'Currencies: Strength in reserve', *Financial Times*, 8 February 2011.

Beattie, A. and Q. Peel (2010) 'Scene set for G20 battle over fiscal strategy', *Financial Times*, 24 June 2010.

Bénassy-Quéré, A. and J. Pisani-Ferry (2011) 'What International Monetary System For a Fast-Changing World Economy', Working Paper 2011/06, Bruegel, Brussels, April.

Bergsten, F. C. (2009) 'We should listen to Beijing's currency idea', *Financial Times*, 8 April 2009.

Bernanke, B. S. (2010) 'Rebalancing the Global Recovery', Sixth European Central Bank Central Banking Conference, Frankfurt, 19 November 2010.

Bini-Smaghi, L. (2006) 'Powerless Europe: Why is the Euro Area Still a Political Dwarf?', *International Finance*, 9 (2), 261–79.

Blyth, M. (2002) *Great Transformations: Economic Ideas and Institutional Change in the Twentieth Century*, Cambridge, Cambridge University Press.

Blyth, M. (2003) 'The Political Power of Financial Ideas: Transparency, Risk, and Distribution in Global Finance', in J. Kirshner (ed.) *Monetary Orders: Ambiguous Economics, Ubiquitous Politics*, Ithaca, Cornell University Press.

Calleo, D. P. (2009) 'Twenty-First Century Geopolitics and the Erosion of the Dollar Order, in E. Helleiner & J. Kirshner (eds) (2009) *The Future of the Dollar*, Ithaca (NY), Cornell University Press.

Cao, H. (2009) Interview with author, Institute of Finance and Banking, Chinese Academy of Social Sciences, Beijing, 19 May 2009.

Chin, G. and E. Helleiner (2008) 'China as a Creditor: A Rising Financial Power?', *Journal of International Affairs*, 62 (1), 87–102.

Chin, G. and Y. Wang (2010) 'Debating the International Currency System', *China Security*, 6 (1), 3–20.

Cohen, B. J. (2006a) 'The Macrofoundations of Monetary Power', in D. M. Andrews (ed.) *International Monetary Power*, Cornell University Press, 31–50.

Cohen, B. J. (2006b) 'The Euro and Transatlantic Relations' in Thomas L. Ilgen (ed.) *Hard Power, Soft Power and the Future of Transatlantic Relations*, Aldershot, Ashgate, 73–89.

Cohen, B. J. (2008a) 'The International Monetary System: Diffusion and Ambiguity', *International Affairs*, 84 (3), 455–70.

Cohen, B. J. (2008b) *Global Monetary Governance*, London, Routledge.

Cohen, B. J. (2009) 'Toward a Leaderless Currency System', in E. Helleiner & J. Kirshner (eds) *The Future of the Dollar*, Ithaca (NY), Cornell University Press, 142–63.

Cohen, B. J. (2010) *The Future of Global Currency: The Euro Versus the Dollar*, London, Routledge.

Cookson, R. and G. Dyer (2010) 'Currencies: Yuan direction', *Financial Times*, 13 December 2010.

Cooper, R. (2011) 'Is SDR Creation Inflationary?' Independent External Consultant Paper to the International Monetary Fund, Washington, 7 January 2011. <http://www.imf.org/external/np/pp/eng/2011/010711a.pdf>.

De la Dehesa, G. (2009) 'Will the Euro Ever Replace the US Dollar as the Dominant Global Currency', Working Paper 54, Royal Elcano Institite, Madrid.

Ding, Y. (2009) Interview with author, Development and Research Centre, Beijing, 7 April 2009.

Dyer, G., J. Anderlini and H. Sender (2011) 'China's lending hits new heights', *Financial Times*, 17 January 2011.

Eichengreen, B. (2007) 'The Misguided Dream of Asian Monetary Union', *Global Asia*, 2 (3), 90–9.

Eichengreen, B. (2008) *Globalizing Capital: A History of International Monetary System*, Princeton and Oxford, Princeton University Press.

Eichengreen, B. (2011) *Exorbitant Privilege: The Rise and Fall of the Dollar*, Oxford and New York, Oxford University Press.

Flynn, D. and K. Yao (2011) 'G20 lays bare different reform agendas at China forum', *Reuters*, 31 March 2011.

Galati, G. and P. D. Wooldrige (2006) 'The Euro as a Reserve Currency: A Challenge to the Pre-eminence of the US Dollar?' BIS Working Papers, 218 December, Basel, Switzerland.

Hall, B. (2010) 'Sarkozy unveils G20 leadership agenda', *Financial Times*, 25 August 2010.

Helleiner, E. (1994) *States and the Reemergence of Global Finance*, Ithaca, Cornell University Press.

Helleiner, E. and J. Kirshner (2009) (eds) *The Future of the Dollar*, Ithaca, Cornell University Press.

Henning, C. R. (1998) 'Systemic Conflict and Regional Monetary Integration: The Case of Europe', *International Organization*, 52 (3), 537–73.
Henning, C. R. (2006) 'The Exchange-Rate Weapon and Macroeconomic Conflict', in D. M. Andrews (ed.) *International Monetary Power*, Cornell University Press, 117–38.
Hollinger, P. and C. Giles (2010) 'France woos China over currency talks', *Financial Times*, 1 October 2010.
International Monetary Fund (IMF) (2010), 'Reserve Accumulation and International Monetary Stability', Strategy, Policy and Review Department, 13 April 2010.
International Monetary Fund (IMF) (2011a) 'Enhancing International Monetary Stability – A Role for the SDR?', Strategy, Policy and Review Department, Washington, IMF, 7 January 2011.
International Monetary Fund (IMF) (2011b) 'IMF Executive Board Meeting on Enhancing International Monetary Stability – A Role for the SDR?', Public Information Notice (PIN) No. 11/22, Washington, IMF, 10 February 2011.
Interview X-3 (2009) Anonymised interview, Beijing, 3 April 2009.
Interview X-10 (2009) Anonymised interview, European Commission Office, Beijing, 22 May 2009.
Interview X-18 (2009) Anonymised interview, Beijing, 22 May 2009.
Interview X-25 (2009) Anonymised interview, Chinese Academy of Social Sciences, Beijing, 23 April 2009.
Jabko, N. (2010) 'The hidden face of the Euro', *Journal of European Public Policy*, 17 (3), 318–34.
Julius, D. (2010) 'A Roadmap for SDR Evolution', in P. Subacchi and J. Driffill (eds) *Beyond the Dollar: Rethinking the International Monetary System*, London, Chatham House.
Kenen, P. (2010) 'An SDR Based Reserve System', *Journal of Globalization and Development*, 1 (2), Art. 13.
Kindleberger, C. P. (1986) *The World in Depression, 1929–39*, Berkley and Los Angeles, University of California Press.
Kindleberger, C. (2000) 'A New Bi-Polarity?' in R. Mundell and A. Clesse (eds) *The Euro as a Stabilizer in the International Economic System*. Dordrecht, Kluwer Academic Publishers.
Kirshner, J. (2009) 'After the (Relative) Fall: Dollar Diminution and the Consequences for American Power', in E. Helleiner and J. Kirshner (eds) *The Future of the Dollar*, Ithaca, Cornell University Press, 191–215.
Krugman, P. (2009) 'China's Dollar Trap', *New York Times*. 2 April 2009.
Lukes, S. (1974) *Power: A Radical View*, London, MacMillan.
Lukes, S. (2005) *Power: A Radical View* (2nd Edition), London, MacMillan.

McKinnon, R. (2010) 'Rehabilitating the Unloved Dollar Standard', Unpublished, February. <http://www.stanford.edu/~mckinnon/papers/unloved_Dollar_standard.pdf>.

Mallet, V. and G. Wiesmann (2011) 'China's Spanish debt buys put at €6bn', *Financial Times*, 6 January 2011.

Marsh, D. (2009) *The Euro: The Politics of the New Global Currency*, New Heaven and London, Yale University Press.

Mundell, R. (2005) 'The case for a world currency', *Journal of Policy Modelling*, 27, 465–75.

Otero-Iglesias, M. (2011) 'The (In)tangible Euro Challenge to the Dollar: Insights from the Financial Elites in Brazil and China', *Cambridge Review of International Affairs*, forthcoming.

Palais-Royal Initiative (PRI) (2011) *Reform of the International Monetary System: A Cooperative Approach for the Twenty First Century*, Paris, 18 January 2011.

Qin Y. (2009) Interview with author, China Foreign Affairs University, Beijing, 13 May 2009.

Reuters (2010) 'China Offers Rare Glimpse Into Reserves, Heavy in Dollars', 3 September 2010.

Rohan, B. and A. Breidthardt (2010) 'Germany says weak US means Europe needs more unity', *Reuters*, 5 November 2010.

Sarkozy, N. (2010) Press conference given after the G20 Seoul summit, 12 November 2010. <http://ambafrance-us.org/spip.php?article1982>.

Savona, P. (2010) 'The Euro and the Greek crisis: a new international monetary scenario' G8-G20 Information Centre, University of Toronto, 16 May 2010. <http://www.g8.utoronto.ca/newsdesk/g8g20/g8g20-savona.html>.

Stiglitz, J. (2009) 'The UN takes Charge', *International Business Times*, 9 July 2009.

Stiglitz, J. and B. Greenwald (2010) 'Towards a New Global Reserve System', *Journal of Globalization and Development*, 1 (2), Art. 10.

Strange, S. (1971) 'The Politics of International Currencies', *World Politics*, 23 (2), 215–31.

Strange, S. (1982) 'Still an Extraordinary Power: America's Role in a Global Monetary System', in R. E. Lombra and W. E. Witte (eds), *Political Economy of International and Domestic Monetary Relations*, Iowa, Iowa State University Press, 73–103.

Strange, S. (1987) 'The Persistent Myth of Lost Hegemony', *International Organization*, 41 (4), 551–74.

Strange, S. (1994) *States and Markets*, London and New York, Continuum.

Subacchi, P. (2010) 'One Currency, Two Systems: China's Renminbi Strategy', Briefing Paper 2010/01, Chatham House, London, October.

Tett, G. and B. Hall (2010) 'Sarkozy calls for action on currencies', *Financial Times*, 27 January 2010.

Thomas, L. (2009) 'Dollar's dominance under fire at G8 summit', *Associate France Press*, 10 July 2009.
Triffin, R. (1960) *Gold and the Dollar Crisis: The Future of Convertibility*, New Haven, Yale University Press.
United Nations (2009) *Preliminary Report of the Commission of Experts on Reforms of the International Monetary and Financial System*, New York, United Nations (May).
United Nations Conference on Trade and Development (UNCTAD) (2009) *Trade and Development Report, 2009*, New York and Geneva, United Nations.
United Nations Conference on Trade and Development (UNCTAD) (2010) 'Global Monetary Chaos', Policy Brief No. 12, New York and Geneva, United Nations.
Vermeiren, M. (2011) 'Monetary Power and Europe: European Autonomy in the Global Monetary System', paper presented at the 2011 Annual Conference of the British International Studies Association, Manchester, 27–9 April 2011.
Vidal-Folch, X. (2009) 'Si Europa no se integra, mandarán EEUU y China' (If Europe does not integrate, the US and China will lead), interview with Jacques Delors, *El País*, 6 December 2009.
Waldmeir, P. (2009) 'Rebuff for EU in push for strong renminbi', *Financial Times*, 29 November.
Wang, X. (2009) 'Big push for global reserve currency', *China Daily*, 31 March 2009.
Webb, J. (2008) 'Dollar crisis looms, China ponders reform: Mundell', *Reuters*, 3 June 2008.
White, G. (2010) 'Soros: China Saved the Euro', *Reuters*, 15 September 2010.
Wolf, M. (2010) 'Why America is going to win the global currency battle', *Financial Times*, 12 October 2010.
Wyplosz, C. (2009) 'The Blessing of Having the Euro and the Need to Make it Better', Working Paper 41, Royal Elcano Institute, Madrid, Spain.
Xinhua (2011) 'Sanya Declaration of the BRICS Leaders Meeting, 14 April 2011.
Xinhua (2007) 'China, EU to jointly avoid fluctuations of exchange rate', 28 November 2007.
Zhang, Ming (2009) 'China's New International Financial Strategy amid the Global Financial Crisis', *China & and the World Economy*, 17 (5), September–October.
Zhang, Monan (2010) 'US-waged war of currencies', *China Daily*, 20 October 2010.
Zhou, X. (2009) 'Reform of the International Monetary System', Speeches, People's Bank of China, 23 March 2009. <http://www.pbc.gov.cn/english/detail.asp?col=6500&id=178>.
Zhou, X. (2011) 'On Savings Ratio', *Financial Stability Review* (Banque de France), 15 February, 165–9.

MARIE-JOSÉ RINALDI-LARRIBE

2 The Role of the Euro as a Global Currency After the 2008 Crisis

Through a first part devoted to the analysis of business cycles evolution since the launching of the European single currency, we seek to determine whether the criteria of the Optimum Currency Area theory were fulfilled by the Euro area until 2008; then the chapter goes on to analyse the impact of the current financial and economic crisis on Euro area members, from an internal angle (has the Euro protected the Euro area economies, or not, and in which respect?) as well as from an external angle (has the Euro been affected in its international role as a global currency by the crisis, or by the way the crisis was dealt with by Member states and European institutions?). Reforms in the European governance and the creation of tools needed to supervise the European banking and financial system and to reinforce the surveillance of budgetary positions in Member states are examined. Scenarios of future developments of the sovereign debt crisis are then discussed, as well as pros and cons of exiting the Euro area, especially for debt-laden countries. Finally, as a lesson of this crisis, how should European governance evolve in the near future?

Introduction

The Optimal Currency Area (OCA) theory states that countries are more suited to belong to a monetary union when they meet certain criteria related to the real convergence of an economy: high degree of external openness, mobility of factors of production, and diversification of production structures. According to this theory, there should be an increasing correlation between the business cycles of the Euro area, if the area is to be judged optimal, because the costs linked to the existence of asymmetric shocks are less likely to be significant. In effect countries benefit from participating in a monetary union if they have similar business cycles, together with high trade links, flexible factor prices and a fiscal transfer mechanism. Similarity of business cycles in turn will decrease the likelihood of occurrence of asymmetric shocks, i.e. shocks that would be country-specific, hurting economies differently.

When the criteria determined by the Optimal Currency Area (OCA) theory are fulfilled, and when the business cycles are found to be correlated between countries, real convergence has thus been achieved. In this contribution, we shall try to find out whether real convergence had increased between economies belonging to the Euro area, from the launch of the Euro until the crisis of 2008, and whether a Euro(pean) business cycle had emerged. Many studies have been made on this issue, using different techniques and with very diverse results. After having reviewed the existing literature devoted to business cycles synchronisation, we shall focus on the pre-crisis period, which clearly shows a diverging evolution of the economies, mostly in terms of public finances, but also in terms of growth and inflation, between core countries and peripheral ones, even though the crisis can be seen as the expression of a common or symmetric shock. We shall see that even though the business cycles of the Euro area members had first been converging mostly prior to 1999, there is a clear opposite trend after 2004, which partly explains why the impact of the crisis differs among member countries. Consequences will be drawn as to a potential optimality of the European Monetary Union according to the OCA theory.

In the second part of this chapter we shall analyze the evolution of the Euro since the beginning of the current financial and economic crisis, from an internal angle: the debt crisis experienced by several countries has led to a major reform of the system, in terms of a better surveillance of the fiscal policies of the Euro zone countries and with the creation of the European Financial Stability Facility and of the European Stability Mechanism. This reform was crucial for the rescue and for the sustainability of the European Monetary Union and we shall observe that many of these risks had been foreseen before the launching of the single currency, when the Maastricht criteria were defined and even more through the adoption of the Growth and Stability Pact. Lessons must be drawn from the crisis, in particular when defining new governance rules for Euro area members.

From an external angle then, the chapter wonders whether the Euro has been affected in its international role as a global currency by the crisis or by the way the crisis was dealt with by Member states and European institutions. We have witnessed an active involvement of China as an investor in several countries' public debt during the crisis, and we shall try to understand the motivation of the Chinese authorities in doing so, and the potential consequences on the international role of the Euro. Finally, the chapter analyzes different scenarios of future development of the debt crisis, as well as pros and cons of remaining in the Euro area.

Has real convergence increased between Euro area economies, from the launching of the Euro until the crisis of 2008, according to the OCA theory?

Maastricht criteria are related to nominal convergence; real convergence needs to be assessed considering other criteria, among which those developed by the Optimal Currency Area (OCA) theory; this theory was implemented in the 1960s by Robert Mundell,[1] and enriched both by Ronald Mac Kinnon (1963) and Peter Kenen (1969). In order for a monetary union to be qualified as optimal, countries that belong to this area should fulfil several criteria, such as the degree of openness of the country, its industrial diversification and the mobility of production factors; indeed, factor markets must be sufficiently flexible to absorb shocks in a context where exchange rate movements are no longer possible. The two first criteria seem to be fulfilled: Euro area countries are open economies,

1 R. Mundell (1961); R. Mundell (1997).

and they trade more and more with each other. Moreover, we can observe an increasing diversification of production structures in the Euro area. Besides, according to the endogenous cycle's hypothesis of Frankel and Rose (1998), a rise in trade relations enabled by the accession to the Euro area tends to strengthen the synchronisation of cycles, which 'increases the aptitude of countries which, *ex ante*, do not satisfy the criteria of entry in the monetary union, to satisfy them *ex post*'. Nevertheless, Frankel and Rose point out that when countries have not finished the first phase of the transition yet (relative price restructuring and economic growth recovery), a strategy of anchorage can reveal itself counter-productive. As explained by Babetskii (2004), the endogeneity argument described by Frankel and Rose (1998) can illustrate the position taken by the European Commission in 2000, for which 'closer integration leads to less frequent asymmetric shocks and to more synchronised business cycles between countries', which in turn makes it possible and less costly for a common monetary policy to operate; on the contrary, according to what De Grauwe (1997) has called the 'Krugman view', Krugman (1993) believes that closer integration leads to higher specialisation which in turn brings about more idiosyncratic shocks. Babetskii has tested both views and finds that 'an increase in trade intensity leads to higher symmetry of demand shocks' and that 'a decrease in exchange rate volatility has a positive effect on demand shock convergence', which tends to support Frankel and Rose's analysis; concerning supply shocks, the results appear to be ambiguous or non significant. Rose (2000) has demonstrated later on that currency unions increased trade in participating countries by 300% on average; Micco, Stein and Ordonez (2003) confirm that joining a European currency union leads to a surge in trade by 4 to 16%; moreover they find that the microeconomic benefits of the European monetary union are higher than the macroeconomic cost of losing the monetary instrument.

On the other hand, Berger and Nitsch (2006) find that the Euro has had no real effect on trade among members; instead they point out the existence of a gradual increase in trade intensity throughout the fifty years of continued European integration, which culminates with the birth of the single currency. Moreover, Lane (2006) argues that even though there is increasing evidence that the monetary union has increased trade and financial integration among participants, structural rigidities in the labour and goods markets stay, and 'it remains an open question whether national economies will prove to be sufficiently flexible to enable smooth adjustment in the event of a major asymmetric shock or a financial crisis'; moreover, the author believes that 'EMU acts as an amplification mechanism for asymmetric shocks', in the sense that a common nominal interest rate automatically leads to a divergence in real interest rates in members of the Euro area, because of differences in national inflation rates. For Van De Coevering (2003) from an OCA perspective most countries in the Euro area have diverged instead of converging, since the mid-nineties. When studying the correlation of supply and demand shocks between New Member States and the Euro area countries through the 1990s, Firdnuc and Korhonen (2001) come up with several interesting findings: in particular they confirm that members of the Euro area present a high correlation, even Italy which is considered as 'peripheral'. De Haan, Inklaar and Jong-a-Pin (2005) provide a very useful survey of the empirical research on business cycle synchronisation, which reminds us that although periods of bigger and lower synchronisation tend to alternate, there is nonetheless some evidence of greater business cycle synchronisation in the Euro area during the 1990s. However, they also mention the fact that conclusions derived from various studies often differ because of differences in periods surveyed, data and benchmarks used; even when the same methodology is used, results can differ widely. They also find that the synchronisation process has indeed increased, during the 1990s, due to higher trade intensity; they point out that although many Euro area countries' business cycles are still different, there seems to be 'a monotone movement towards the emergence of a European business cycle'. For Bower and Guillemineau (2006) as well, the implementation of the single European market has increased trade relations across Euro area countries, since the 1980s until 2004, which has contributed to higher business cycle symmetry; this has been reinforced by the introduction of the single currency, which has led to intensified intra-trade industry, or similarity of trade specialisation patterns; these findings support the conclusion of Frankel and Rose (1998), with their endogeneity criterion.

On the contrary Artis (2003) indicates that it is difficult to identify 'a homogenous or developing European business cycle' and that 'globalisation may be proceeding as fast as Europeanisation'; the author uses GDP data for a panel of 23 countries, over a 30 year time-frame, and finds out that the US and Japan are sometimes more closely linked to European core countries, than other European countries (such as Great Britain, Portugal, Ireland or Scandinavian countries). For Artis, it means that there is no monotone movement 'towards the emergence of a highly coherent and exclusive European cycle'. We can see that the existence of a real European business cycle is still open to debate.

For Darvas and Szapary (2004), some evidence is found of a high synchronisation of business cycles among Euro area members. Similarly according to Altavilla (2004), since the Maastricht Treaty, EMU members' business cycles have moved closer: 'severe monetary and fiscal discipline has led to an increase in the business cycle affiliation of the participating economies' and there is a 'common cycle driving macroeconomic activity in Europe'. Darvas, Rose and Szapary (2005) then show by using data from 21 OECD countries that reduced fiscal deficits increase business cycle synchronisation; in that sense, the Maastricht criteria might have 'indirectly moved Europe closer to an OCA, by reducing countries' abilities to create idiosyncratic fiscal shocks'. For Mink, Jacobs and De Haan (2007), even if some countries have seen their business cycle become increasingly similar to the Euro area business cycle (France, Germany and the Netherlands), in general the evolution of business cycles in EMU remains rather different, in particular in Italy, Finland and Greece. For Gayer (2007) who uses cross-country correlations, the mean level of synchronisation within the Euro area since 1999 is high overall, except for 2003, though 'not higher than in the first half of the nineties'; according to Gayer, there is a distinct Euro area cycle, 'though evidence for a further increase in synchronisation since the introduction of the Euro is sparse'. Finally, Aguiar-Conraria and Soares (2011) state that Germany, France, Spain, Austria and the Benelux countries form the core of the Euro area, whereas other Euro area members are still in the process of converging (especially Ireland and Italy); as to Portugal, it is clearly lagging behind. Consequently we can see that, contrary to chapters written at the end of the 1990s or beginning of the

2000 decade, recent studies do not necessarily conclude that business cycles of Euro area members converge; they often emphasise the fact that a distinction needs to be made between two or three groups of countries. More importantly, these studies show that when there is an increase in business cycle synchronisation, it is at least partly due to monetary and fiscal discipline, which means that it is applicable before 2003–4. Indeed, when fiscal discipline disappears, as it was the case in some Euro area members, synchronisation becomes less obvious.

A report from the Zentrum für Europäische Wirtschaftsforschung (ZEW)[2] made in November 2008 for the European Commission came to the same conclusion: it stated that the analysis of output gaps is the best indicator of business cycle synchronisation between economies: it can define clusters with countries sharing comparable business cycle characteristics. As the report points out, even though the literature is not absolutely conclusive as to the reason for the higher convergence between Euro area members' business cycles (is it due to the existence of a 'Euro business cycle', or is it linked to the evolution of the World business cycle?), it appears that constraints imposed by the Growth and Stability Pact 'have been found to contribute to business cycle synchronisation'. Can we conclude that the absence of these constraints during a more recent period explains, at least partly, the renewed divergence between those economies? The study observes that contrary to what had happened in the previous years, the increase in correlation has stopped in 2003. Moreover it identified the following clusters: Netherlands, Austria and Germany on the one hand; then Belgium, France, Spain and Italy; and then Greece and Portugal. As to Ireland, Luxembourg and Finland, their evolution is quite different. Besides, on average, there is a higher synchronisation between business cycles of countries located at the centre of the Euro area than between business cycles of peripheral countries. The results of the cluster analysis provided by this study show that 'bilateral trade intensity and common borders are more important determinants of business cycle synchronisation than the institutional environment, fiscal policies, or the industry structure of the

2 Centre for European Economic Research, Mannheim and Vienna.

countries in consideration'. Still, fiscal policy seems to be important, which means that fiscal convergence fosters business cycle synchronisation. Finally, the authors of this report conclude that 'the business cycle synchronisation in the Euro area itself is at a high level without a clear trend of increasing or decreasing' and that 'the introduction of the Euro has been conducive to low and stable output and inflation dispersion but perhaps at the cost of some increase in fiscal dispersion'.

On the contrary, the Deutsche Bank Research (2006) describes a monotonous increase in the average correlation among GDP growth rates of EMU countries, except for Greece, even if it slows down after the creation of the Euro. They conclude that there is a general trend towards greater synchronisation of business cycles in the Euro area. According to P. De Grauwe (2008), instead of a convergence trend we have witnessed a clear divergence movement in Euro area countries, in terms of inflation (although price convergence had been observed prior to 1999) as well as in terms of labour costs; some countries have seen their unit labour costs increase (Portugal, Netherlands, Spain and Italy) whereas these costs have drastically been reduced in Germany and Austria; competitive positions of Eurozone countries have thus sharply diverged. As De Grauwe explains, 'there has been a coordination failure in the Eurozone. There can be no doubt that this had led to a major asymmetric shock that will have to be corrected'; indeed it is being corrected sharply in the countries that currently have to bear the costs of an austerity plan.

Regling, Deroose, Felke and Kutos (2010) confirm that although EMU has brought substantial benefits to its members, imbalances within the Euro area have also grown a lot during the decade of existence of the single currency, in terms of growth, inflation, competitiveness, current accounts and public finances. They add that even though the Euro has protected EMU members during the current economic crisis, the latter has also made this divergence and its consequences even more evident and challenging. Nevertheless, according to the authors, 'the crisis has made EMU even more, not less, attractive, and most EU countries that are not yet members of EMU are keen to join in the foreseeable future'. Besides, 'with the necessary political will, the crisis can be a catalyst for deeper and broader economic coordination and surveillance in the Euro area'.

This review of the literature devoted to OCA theory shows that a Euro area business cycle tends to emerge, at least until 2003–4, but that we tend to observe a diverging trend among Euro area members since then, in terms of growth rates, inflation rates and current account balances, as shown in table 2 and 3 in the appendices; and of course public finances start to deviate again (table 1). Nevertheless, even though it is difficult to assert that EMU is an optimum currency area, especially nowadays, and although we know that the creation of EMU was a political decision, it will certainly move closer to an OCA over time, due to the existence of the endogeneity criterion and due to recent and current reforms.

The impact of the current financial and economic crisis on Euro area members

We shall now analyse the impact of the current financial and economic crisis on Euro area members, from an internal angle; in particular, we shall try to determine whether the Euro has protected Euro area economies or not, and in which respect. Moreover the debt crisis experienced by several countries has led to a major reform of the system, as we shall see later on. This reform was crucial for the rescue and for the sustainability of the European Monetary Union. Many of these risks had been foreseen before the launching of the single currency, when defining the Maastricht criteria and even more through the adoption of the Growth and Stability Pact. Lessons will have to be drawn from the crisis, in particular when defining new governance rules for Euro area members.

There are institutional weaknesses in the Euro area: monetary policy has been handed over to the European Central Bank while fiscal policy is still in the hands of national authorities, which creates the ground for a divergence of public finances among economies of the Euro area. Besides the inflation rates have continued to differ across countries, which have rendered the operation of monetary policy very difficult for the ECB, since the real interest rate has differed strongly at times among countries.[3] Concerning the diverging fiscal policies of Euro area members, the Growth and Stability Pact had however been created in 1997 in order to prevent the occurrence of this situation but the insistence of France and Germany to reform it in 2005 have proven very detrimental since it has enabled countries to increase public deficits and public debt more than they should have. The mechanisms had been put in place on purpose, to avoid countries from taking some distance with the Maastricht criteria once they had adopted the Euro; yet the rules were not followed and the sanctions were removed from the Pact. Moreover, countries' authorities should have followed countercyclical policies during periods of growth, allowing for greater expenses when the situation would reverse; unfortunately in most countries, fiscal policies have been largely procyclical. On the other hand, according to De Grauwe (2008), national politicians still bear the full responsibility for bad trends in unemployment, although the instruments needed to deal with this issue have been transferred to European institutions that have no political responsibility for decisions taken. Nevertheless, for De Grauwe, the 'long run success of the Eurozone depends on the continuing process of political unification (which) is needed to reduce the scope for the emergence of asymmetric shocks and to embed the Eurozone in a wider system of strong political ties that are needed to take care of the inevitable divergent economic movements within the Eurozone'.

In particular, we observe that in the Euro area large current account imbalances have been accumulated after countries had adopted the Euro. In effect, some countries exhibit large current account surpluses in 2002–8 (Germany, the Netherlands, Finland, Luxembourg and Austria), whereas other countries have large current account deficits (Greece, Portugal, Ireland and Spain, as well as new Member states having adopted the Euro), the third group comprising countries with weak export performance and worsening

3 Table 1 in the appendices: countries such as Finland, Luxembourg, Spain, exhibit public surpluses, whereas others like Portugal and Greece have huge public deficits; in 2006 eight countries out of fifteen in the Euro area breach the public debt criterion of 60% of GDP.

current account balances (Belgium, France and Italy).[4] In Spain, the build-up of financial and macroeconomic imbalances is linked to the fact that the boom of the construction sector enabled by the existence of low real interest rates and the attitude of the financial sector, actually led to a sharp rise in real estate prices and to a surge in private debt finally followed by a downturn when credit conditions suddenly changed with the outbreak of the crisis.

Nevertheless, the Euro has limited the impact of the crisis on the economies of the Euro zone; of course the financial crisis has hit all countries, with a severe contraction in GDP for some of them (Greece, Spain, Portugal and Italy, especially in 2012), but most of the Euro area countries did not experience either a huge financial turmoil or a sharp debt crisis, even among the new comers. In particular countries have not experienced exchange rate turbulences, although these had been frequent in the past; moreover, fiscal consolidation when adopting the Euro has given most of the Euro area members a certain room for manoeuvre in order to deal with the crisis. The situation of Greece, Ireland, Spain and Portugal, which had very specific and different issues to deal with, would probably have been much more dramatic, if they had not joined the Euro area. Surely, their currency would have depreciated strongly, but this is not necessarily beneficial for the economy if it happens at a large scale, as shown by the 1992–3 monetary crisis of the EU, when all currencies except the Deutsche Mark had to leave the European Monetary System because they were attacked on financial markets. A recession followed this episode of intense monetary turmoil. There are many similar crises in the economic history of Asia, Latin America and Russia that allow us to conclude that, even though a prolonged overvaluation of a currency can indeed hurt an economy or a group of economies, a sharp depreciation of a currency can be even more detrimental. Of course the Euro may currently be overvalued; nevertheless, if we have a global view of the evolution of the Euro vis-à-vis the main currencies, in particular the US dollar, the single currency has reached higher levels in the past (it was close to 1.60$ on 15 July 2008, as shown on Figure 1).

4 Table 3 in the appendices.

Of course, peripheral countries that have seen their competitiveness decrease over the past years would be better off with a slight depreciation of the Euro, even if we know that Euro area countries' exports are mainly directed toward other Euro area countries, or toward European countries but invoiced in Euro.

As mentioned by Regling, Deroose, Felke and Kutos (2010), new Member states which have joined the Euro area (Malta, Cyprus, Slovenia, Slovakia) have been shielded from the impact of the financial turmoil (at least until 2012 for Cyprus) and they have not suffered from liquidity shortages; the Euro 'has thus acted as an umbrella against possible liquidity strains that would otherwise have affected the smaller, and less-credible, pre-Euro currencies'. Besides, the long-term borrowing environment of the Euro-area is still a major benefit for debt-burdened peripheral countries, because in another context they might have been faced with even higher interest rates 'to compensate for the higher credit default and exchange rate risk'. It is true on the other hand, if we come back to OCA criteria, that countries that face a deteriorating competitiveness should see a decrease in their wage levels and social standards which would be sufficient enough to compensate for the missing monetary tool, i.e. a devaluation. The austerity measures taken to lower the public deficit in several countries include cuts in wages of public servants that will lead to a decrease in consumer spending, which in turn may lead to a slavish growth, and to lower revenues for the state's budget, creating a vicious circle. Some economists argue that it would be better for Greece to leave EMU for example, and to re-establish a new devalued currency.[5] Others do not believe in the scenario of a break-up of the Euro area but argue that the governance of the area is weak, preventing the Euro from becoming a truly global currency.[6] Later on we shall discuss the potential consequences for a country that would leave the Euro area.

Overall, the European institutions together with the Euro area members have been able to create the mechanisms needed to alleviate the sovereign debt crisis and to improve governance in the Euro area. They have

5 Hankel, Nölling and Schachtschneider (2010).

6 Pisani-Ferry, Sapir (2009).

decided to strengthen the surveillance of Euro area economies and to ensure that these economies converge, through a better coordination of their economic policies. As mentioned previously, mechanisms did exist in order to prevent a divergence in public finances in Euro area countries: the Maastricht Treaty had provided a framework for surveillance and the Stability and Growth Pact (SGP) was supposed to make the Maastricht rules permanent, regarding public finances, but it was reformed and the sanctions removed. France, Italy and Germany, which did not abide by these rules anymore, were able to convince other countries to reform the SGP, thus removing the possibility for the European Commission to apply a financial penalty against countries which did not comply with the rules. From that moment, the situation was likely to deteriorate and it has led to the coexistence in the Euro area of very diverse situations with regard not only to the evolution of economic growth, inflation and current account imbalances, but mainly regarding budget deficits and public debt.[7] The crisis has therefore been worsened by the fact that some States have changed the rules of the game, when it suited them the most.

The origin of the crisis lies, as we know, in the U. S. subprime crisis, combined with the unwise attitude of the bankers that rushed towards collateralised debt instruments for which they did not know the exact origin, which required a massive government intervention in order to save the whole banking system from collapse. We can also explain the very rapid spread of the crisis in Europe, enabled by the increasing financial market integration that ultimately created a domino effect or snowball effect that made the crisis even worse. This is the reason why the idea according to which the crisis would mean the end of the Euro seems excessive and unjustified for the following reasons: the crisis started in the United States and resulted from the conjunction between a low interest rate policy put in place by the Federal Reserve at the end of 2001 and the deregulation policy led by G. W. Bush, which has encouraged the housing bubble and an increasing private debt. Irresponsible behaviour and the blindness of some bankers have then contributed to the rapid explosion of the financial crisis and to

7 See Table 1 and 2 in the appendices.

its spread to the real economy, creating the biggest recession the world has known since the 1930s. Blaming the Euro for this crisis seems quite exaggerated! Reforms have been and must continue to be implemented for a better functioning of EMU, since we know that the creation of a single currency generates a number of constraints necessary for the stability of the system: it is essential that Member states control their public finances in times of growth in order to be able to increase public expenditure when a shock affects the economy. But regularly announcing the end of the Euro is not a reasonable attitude. Rather it is a signal for all actors at stake, European institutions and Heads of State and government to act promptly by taking the necessary measures in order to make the Euro system stable and safe, by increasing supervision and systemic risk surveillance, and by creating mechanisms through which countries under financial stress will be able to finance their public deficit. The build-up of huge public debts in the peripheral countries of the EU, such as Greece, Ireland, Portugal, Italy, but also in France, has created a distrust of economic agents and financial markets, and a sovereign debt crisis that we had never experienced in Europe. Spanish leaders for their part have not paid enough attention to the creation of this huge housing bubble, combined with a surge in households' private debt. For Ireland it is the poor governance of the financial sector, coupled with a property bubble that lie at the origin of the country's difficulties. Rating agencies have then amplified the crisis, generating a panic in financial markets, and literally leading to a surge in the financing cost for some countries. According to the Economist Intelligence Unit (2011), the roots of the European crisis lie in the fact that 'profligacy' in the periphery of the Euro area was funded by carefulness in the core countries: this informal deal suited both sides at the beginning: 'while countries in the periphery enjoyed debt-fuelled booms, countries such as Germany, where domestic demand was weak, could rely on exports to keep growing'.

It seems like the greatest successes in terms of European integration are unfortunately obtained in times of crises. As already mentioned, the mechanisms which are essential to the survival of a single currency were known to all, but they were not in place at the right moment: in the absence of a federal budget, the Euro area was in need of a kind of European Monetary Fund, modelled on the IMF, for countries that need to be able to finance their public debt at a lower cost, while pledging to put their public finances in order. Moreover the European Commission should have monitored the public accounts of the Euro area economies more closely, thus avoiding any attempt of cheating by a country, as it was the case twice with Greece. The convergence criteria were included in the Maastricht Treaty so that the economies of the Euro area would converge before adopting the Euro, which they managed to do; then economies have started to diverge again, as we have seen. It is difficult for the ECB to conduct a single monetary policy when economies diverge.

Reforms adopted since the beginning of the crisis

In June 2010, European institutions and Heads of State and government put in place an emergency mechanism for countries to finance their public debts while reassuring the markets: the European Financial Stability Facility. This facility allows the EU to raise funds on financial markets, which are guaranteed by the European budget and by Member states, and to lend these funds to countries in need at a reasonable interest rate, in exchange for the countries' commitment to take necessary measures to improve their fiscal position. The European Financial Stability Facility represented at first a total of 440 billion Euro, adding to a community fund of 60 billion Euro created to support the Euro area countries, through which the Commission may itself grant loans to troubled countries. Besides, the International Monetary Fund has committed to support countries in the Euro area up to 250 billion Euro. In December 2010, it was decided that the EFSF would be replaced by a permanent system, the European Stability Mechanism, by July 2012, requiring an amendment to the Treaty on the Functioning of the European Union, therefore imposing State ratification. Then the overall ceiling for the EFSF/ESM was raised to 700 billion Euro according to a decision by the Eurogroup taken on 30 March 2012, the ESM being used to finance new programs as from July 2012, and the EFSF concerning programs already put in place.

In June 2013, Eurozone finance ministers agreed that the ESM would also be allowed to invest in troubled banks (up to 60 billion Euro), if conditions were met, in order to disconnect banks from governments. Of course the government would first have to recapitalise the bank until it meets the minimum common equity Tier 1 ratio of 4.5%. As the Eurogroup President, J. Dijsselbloem, declared, 'this instrument will help preserve the stability of the Euro area and remove the risk of contagion of the financial sector to the sovereign'.[8]

To deal with the crisis, governments have also taken measures to regulate financial activities, since we know that speculators have been actors of the contagion of the debt crisis. A rise in interest rates on the debts of countries in difficulty results in lower rates for safer countries, which means that if a fund invests in German government bonds, it will be even better off if troubled countries are struggling to finance their debt! Furthermore, derivatives such as short selling and CDS (credit default swaps) only encourage speculation, fuelling the crisis. It was therefore crucial to take measures to make financial activities more transparent, strengthening the monitoring of credit developments and the process of debt securitisation. The European Commission has been warning that the integration of European financial markets would require a better cross-border mechanism for prudential supervision, crisis management and resolution, but more than ten years after the launching of the Euro, supervision remains 'largely fragmented along national lines despite the ever-growing importance of cross-border financial activity, including the pan-European trading of sophisticated financial products'.[9] Three European supervisory authorities and a European Committee of systemic risk were thus created at the end of 2010. Derivatives have not been prohibited due to a lack of consensus among different countries, but they can temporarily be suspended under exceptional circumstances.

A Banking Union is also in the process of being implemented, with the creation of a Single Supervisory Mechanism in June 2013. The single supervisory mechanism (SSM) will be monitored by the European Central Bank thus strengthening the Economic and Monetary Union. It is a first step

8 'Ministers put straitjacket on bailout fund', Euractiv.com, 21 June 2013.

9 Regling, Deroose, Felke and Kutos (2010).

towards an integrated 'banking union' which should comprise other elements such as a single rulebook (a regulation giving more power to the ECB for the supervision of banks in the Euro area), a common deposit protection and a single bank resolution mechanism (SRM). The European Banking Authority will continue to coordinate and supervise banks from all European countries. This creates some tensions with the UK, which has its own supervisory body and fears interference from the European Central Bank.

As to the European Central Bank, it has demonstrated its determination to fight against the financial crisis by providing massive amounts of liquidity in the interbank market, in order to encourage banks to continue financing the economies, and by purchasing massive amounts of bonds from countries weakened by the debt crisis. In effect, the ECB has tried to alleviate the crisis by cutting its intervention rate and by providing liquidity at the midst of the financial crisis in order to relieve the interbank market; it then began purchasing bonds on secondary markets, from countries such as Greece, Ireland and Portugal, which were facing great difficulties to refinance their debt (Italy and Spain too, in August 2011). The ECB's sovereign bond purchase programme, named SMP (Securities Market Programme), has been questioned by some central bankers and analysts; nevertheless, it has also been praised by others, especially by Members of the European Parliament. The SMP was then replaced in September 2012 by a new programme entitled Outright Monetary Transactions (OMT). Moreover, more than 1000 billion Euro have been provided to the market through Long-Term Refinancing Operations (LTRO), while collateral rules were loosened. This provision of liquidity has alleviated the pressure on the interbank market, preventing a major credit crunch and bringing down yields on Euro zone bond markets (although part of the liquidity has been deposited with the ECB instead of going into the real economy).[10] In the end, inflation has been contained and the Euro system has not collapsed.

An issue which remains unsettled is the creation of Eurobonds in the Euro area, for which States have not reached an agreement yet; these bonds could correspond to a maximum of 60% of the total debt of a country, which would allow the country to benefit from a low rate of interest since

10 Suranyi (2012).

it would be backed with a guarantee from other countries in the Euro area (for which the overall rating would therefore be better). Of course, before launching Eurobonds, a necessary precondition would be the possibility for the European Commission to control the public accounts of the Members of the Euro area, in order to avoid the emergence of diverging situations in terms of public finance. Fiscal integration or the adoption of debt limits in Member states' constitutions would be even more crucial. But Germany does not support this kind of device, which is presented by many analysts as a possible and logical solution. The adoption of the European Financial Stability Facility was the first step towards fiscal integration, since it has provided loans to Ireland, Portugal and Greece; the creation of common Eurobonds would represent the following step, even though the cost for Germany has been estimated at around 47 billion Euro a year, because of the slight increase in the interest rate offered for these bonds, that Germany would face compared to the current rate.[11] Ultimately the creation of these Eurobonds would enable to narrow debt spreads, since it would enable countries to finance most of their debt at a much lower rate; only an incremental part of the debt would be subject to higher interest rates, reassuring investors.

Obviously the right balance needs to be found between implementation of austerity measures that will convince markets that the country is making enough efforts to restore its credibility through sounder public finances, and the realistic view that too much austerity may hinder economic recovery and thus fulfilment of the fiscal objectives. In effect, an important issue that still needs to be tackled is the relevance and the appropriateness of such austerity programmes in countries that are completely incapable of raising their public revenues, and where public spending has already been slashed; Greece for example is likely not to fulfil its promises, if Greek GDP continues to decrease, despite the 'hair-cut' of its debt by 100 billion Euro agreed in October 2011. Can austerity measures restore confidence, thus reducing sovereign spreads, when at the same time we doubt that these measures will enable the Greek economy to achieve

11 'What will Eurobonds cost?', Ifo Institute, 17 August 2011.

economic growth? Could Europeans decide to speed up the implementation of programmes financed by structural funds in particular, in order to boost growth in troubled countries, so as to compensate for the cuts in national spending? In October 2010 the Commission published a report on the role of the EU cohesion policy in dealing with the economic crisis. In July 2009, it was proposing a simplification of the management of the European Funds to help regions to tackle the crisis. Project bonds designed to boost investment in regions have also been discussed. Another solution would be for Germany to stimulate its economy, through a raise in public spending which would lead to an increased internal consumption and thus would help other European countries. Germany had a budgetary surplus representing 0.2% of its GDP in 2012, compared to an average public deficit 3.7% of GDP for the Euro area (Table 1), which leaves some fiscal room for manoeuvre, even if the German public debt still reaches 81.9% of GDP. But this would be contrary to the discipline and philosophy of the German taxpayer. A Member of the European Parliament, Sylvie Goulard, states that 'the Euro will fully benefit from the advantages of its international role when a liquid and global bond market equivalent to the US T-bond market exists'.[12] Unfortunately, Heads of State and government tend to prefer the intergovernmental solution instead of the federal one.

A yearly cycle of economic policy coordination called the European Semester was also put in place because what is needed is coordination among Euro area members on fiscal policy and also on matters related to labour markets and social policy, tax issues and pensions. But more importantly, on 2 March 2012, a new Treaty on Stability, Cooperation and Governance in the Economic and Monetary Union, also called Fiscal Treaty, was signed by 25 countries (the UK and the Czech Republic excluded). The aim is to reinforce budgetary discipline among participating countries, as well as to strengthen the coordination of economic policies and improve the governance of the Euro area. Countries thereby accept to reach a budgetary position which is balanced or in surplus; a structural deficit of 0.5% of GDP is acceptable and can reach 1% of GDP if public debt is below 60% of GDP.

12 'Qui parle au nom de l'Euro ?', Les Echos, 29 June 2011.

If the public debt is beyond this limit the country should reduce it by one twentieth per year. If the country does not comply with its obligations, the European Court of Justice can take action by requesting the imposition of financial sanctions (up to 0.1% of the country's GDP). Finally, the Treaty mentions that countries will have to foster competitiveness and promote employment, 'contributing further to the sustainability of public finances and reinforcing financial stability'. The Treaty entered into force on 1 January 2013, reaffirming the principles of the GSP; it appears quite flexible since it allows countries to define measures that need to be taken in the medium term to reach the goal of a balanced budgetary position, leaving it up to the European Council to decide whether action needs to be taken; at the same time, discipline is reaffirmed through precise rules and possible sanctions, which should encourage contracting parties to implement sound policies.

Finally, several measures were also taken concerning the macroeconomic surveillance and the supervision of the financial system. Indicators such as trade deficit, inflation, unemployment rate, and the evolution of the balance of payments will be analysed closely, in order to prevent the existence of imbalances and bubbles. Sanctions may be applied to countries which would not meet their commitments. The creation of a European rating agency was discussed and stress tests were carried out in order to test the soundness of banks in the event of a new financial shock. In addition, the European Commission should continue to promote free trade and free competition between countries, encouraging them to fight against the temptation of a return to protectionism, which would cause more damage than benefits to European economies; it has been shown that protectionism during the Great Depression had made the situation even worse in industrialised countries. We know that open markets and competition are favourable factors for economic growth: they lead to innovation and progress, and allow companies to achieve economies of scale and improve their competitiveness; moreover it enables consumers to have access to a wider variety of products at lower prices.

As we have already mentioned, the Euro area has gone through a period of severe turbulence, for the first time in its history, but the Member states of the Euro area and the European institutions have been able to put in place the mechanisms required to preserve the Euro system and to help

Member states to deal with the crisis. However, decisions are sometimes taken in a reactive rather than in a proactive way, which is damaging.

Today, we have a clear illustration of the fact that major progress in terms of European integration is often achieved during periods of turmoil. What remains unclear nonetheless is the governance issue created by the existence of new institutions or bodies that intervene in Euro area countries but not in all EU countries (bank supervision). As to the fiscal Treaty it was also ratified by only 25 countries among which all Eurozone members as well as non-Eurozone countries which have decided to abide by the same rules. On the contrary, the European Semester, introduced in January 2011, which enables economic coordination, applies to every Member states, not only to Euro zone members. Clearly we are more and more heading towards an EU '*à la carte*', with countries following different integration rhythms, as we already witnessed with the Schengen area and with the single currency. The system of enhanced cooperation introduced by the Treaty on the European Union or Treaty of Maastricht, reaffirmed in the Lisbon Treaty, makes it possible indeed for countries wishing closer integration to advance at a different pace. As a consequence of this enhanced cooperation procedure, and with the existence of opting-outs in certain domains, governance might become more complex with time.

Has the Euro been affected in its international role as a global currency by the crisis, or by the way the crisis was dealt with by Member states and European institutions?

The role of the Euro as a global currency has increased until 2009, mainly as a reserve currency owned by the major central banks, but also as a currency in which debts are issued and as an invoicing currency. Since 2009 nevertheless its share has decreased in all categories. From a peak of 27.7% in 2009, it now represents 23.9% of the declared official reserves of Central

Banks.[13] Still the Euro has become a global currency in that it represents 22% of the foreign assets of the non-resident banks.[14] Moreover it is one of the most commonly used currencies in transactions on the foreign exchange market and its share increases constantly (from 39.1% in 2009 to 41.2% in 2012, against 86% for the dollar). In terms of stock of international debt securities, the Euro represents 25.5% of the total, against 52.4% for the US currency.[15] According to Lemoine (2011) the Euro serves as an anchor to 48 currencies, whereas the dollar is an anchor to 51 currencies. Furthermore, the difference in the monetary policies implemented by the Federal Reserve and by the ECB can only reinforce the global role of the Euro; in effect the US Central bank has chosen, through the successive quantitative easing measures that were taken, to buy US Treasury bonds without any sterilisation, which has resulted in an increase in the monetary basis. In contrast the ECB has intervened in a more prudent manner, sterilising its interventions in order to avoid a surge in the inflation rate and to guarantee the long-term predictability and stability of the single European currency.

Nevertheless, the sovereign debt crisis has affected the Euro in its role as an international currency as figures stated above show. There has been a loss in confidence from investors, especially in the height of the crisis, in 2011. Since the ECB started to intervene more decisively on the monetary markets and through bond purchases, the confidence partially returned in the second semester of 2012, according to the ECB (2013).

A report by Frankel and Chinn in 2005 had pointed out that if all EU countries were to join the Euro area including the UK, by 2020, then the Euro would overtake the dollar within a few years; the depreciation trend of the dollar observed in 2005, added to the current account deficits and rising international indebtedness of the US toward the rest of the world, reinforced the authors' opinion that a clear shift would take place in favour of the Euro. Has this statement about the rising role of the Euro changed with the financial crisis and with the sovereign debt crisis in the

13 ECB (2013).

14 Mathilde Lemoine (2011).

15 Table 4 in the appendices.

Euro zone? If we look at Tables 3 and 4 in the appendices, it seems like the share of the Euro in global holdings of foreign exchange reserves has been constantly increasing until 2009, decreasing after that date; at the same time we can witness a decrease in the share of the US dollar except for the year 2011. Conversely, holdings of other currencies tend to increase (British Pounds, Canadian dollars, Swiss Francs, etc.). But the question remains: is the dollar going to depreciate in the future? The President of the Federal Reserve, Ben Bernanke, has reiterated his intention to keep an accommodative stance in the near future, which is not going to lead to an appreciation of the dollar; on the other hand, the problems experienced in the Euro area were not supposed to lead to an appreciation of the Euro. Nevertheless the exchange rate of the Euro vis-à-vis the US dollar remains at a level which some analysts consider rather high. The downgrading of the US debt (from AAA to AA-plus) by the rating agency Standard & Poor's in July 2011 did not have a significant impact on the value of the dollar. But many countries in the Euro zone were downgraded also, which has caused panic in the financial markets. These announces tend to be self-fulfilling: when rating agencies downgrade a country, investors lose faith and sell the country's bonds, generating a rise in the interest rate in order to cover for the extra risk, and confirming the signal of the debt crisis to the market. Let's remember that these agencies had not been able to forecast the subprime crisis, giving a triple-A rating to more than 5000 sub-prime instruments; in addition they had no anticipated the bankruptcy of Lehman Brothers, also rated triple-A.

A report issued by Bruegel and by the CEPII in August 2011[16] examines the implications of the likely evolution of the international monetary system and concludes that 'neither the Euro nor the renminbi are in a position to challenge the supremacy of the dollar' even though 'they are likely to play a meaningful international role provided that certain conditions are met', such as reforms made by the Chinese authorities to increase the convertibility of their currency. The report offers three possible scenarios, favouring the first two: in the short and medium term, the report argues

16 Angeloni & al. (2011).

that we should observe a 'repair-and-improve' scenario in which changes and reforms are incremental; in the longer run (10–15 years) a multipolar system structured around two or three international currencies is more likely to emerge. Moreover, according to the authors of the report, 'the capacity of the Euro to increase its international status requires major decisions by the Euro area, such as further governance reform, the creation of a Eurobond market, and the streamlining of external representation'. On the other hand, there is an element that stands in favour of a reinforcement of the international role of the Euro which is linked to the fear of large holders of dollar denominated assets, like China, of a large depreciation of the US currency which would entail a risk of capital losses; this explains their endeavour to rebalance their holdings in favour of the Euro, at least until 2009. But there is a cost attached to the development of the global role of the Euro: international currencies have privileges ('seignoriage' and ability to trade in home currency) as well as duties and costs: 'the main duty of the international reserve-issuer is the responsibility to provide the global economy with international liquidity in times of crisis', and the main cost is associated with a higher volatility of the exchange rate of the global currency due to the likely changes in the demand for assets denominated in this currency. Finally the international role of currencies of emerging countries is less important than the rising role of these countries in the global economy, because of the small size of their financial markets, which exhibit as a consequence an insufficient depth and liquidity. As a consequence, 'as long as access to renminbi-denominated assets remains limited, reserve diversification away from the US dollar risks being overwhelmingly into the Euro'.[17]

Surely an increase in the fiscal integration of the Euro area and the creation of Eurobonds would enable to consolidate the position of the Euro as a global currency. A statement was made in the *Financial Times* by former Heads of government of Italy and Belgium, Giuliano Amato and Guy Verhofstadt, promoting the Eurobond solution, arguing that a certain share of a country's national debt could be converted to EU bonds

17 Angeloni & al. (2011).

on a voluntary basis, which would partially alleviate the crisis. Those EU bond issues 'could be globally traded and would attract surpluses from the central banks of emerging countries and sovereign wealth funds'. They call for a 'New Deal for Europe'.[18] This is all the more essential that Italy saw the yield on its debt rise to more than 6.5% at the end of 2011. We must bear in mind that Italy's public debt is almost three times Spain's and six times Greece's. The ECB has bought for 13.3 billion Euro of Spanish and Italian bonds during the first week of September 2011.

Although we can see that the Euro's role as a global currency used to keep growing, at least until the two last years, Fields and Vernengo (2011) observe that the share of the dollar in official reserves has only decreased by ten percentage points, from 70% in 2001 to 60% in 2010, and that the dollar is still used in most of the international trade transactions. Besides, the leading financial centres are located outside the Euro area. Thus they believe that the dollar is not threatened in its international role and will continue to be the hegemonic currency, because it is 'free of the risk of default' and because the European crisis makes it difficult for the Euro to become a global currency. Still, one can wonder whether their argument is still valid; is the dollar still absolutely 'free of the risk of default'? Of course, the Federal Reserve can continue printing money in order to buy its Treasury bonds, which explains why despite the downgrading made by Standard & Poor's, the US borrowing cost has not increased.

According to Eichengreen (2011a) too, the dollar is likely to maintain its position as the leading global currency in the near future, unless the economic policies implemented by the US authorities would be really bad. Moreover, a devaluation of the dollar is in no one's interest: a renewed strength of the Euro would hurt the recovery in the Euro zone, and would create tensions in Asia, Canada and Australia. As to the renminbi, capital controls limit its attractiveness for the moment, and the Chinese authorities will have to open their financial markets, increase their liquidity and improve the rule of law, before the Chinese currency really becomes an international currency.

18 'A plan to save the Euro, and curb the speculators', *Financial Times*, 4 July 2011.

Yet we have witnessed an active involvement of China as a debt investor in several countries during the crisis. What are the motivations of the Chinese authorities? According to a report from the European Council on Foreign Relations, 'a lack of European cohesion has invited China to deal bilaterally with individual member states to exploit their divisions', and China purchases the bonds of some Member states, because 'it knows that dealing bilaterally with European nations leads to a better pay-off than bolstering multinational initiatives'. Moreover, 'after 2014 – when majority decisions at the European Council will require 15 member states with 65% of the population – it will be useful for the Chinese to have a kind of 'China lobby' consisting of smaller member states. China could always depend on some of them – particularly Malta, Cyprus and Greece – to block any unanimous decision against its interests'. The report also mentions the fact that the use of third-party intermediaries on financial markets by China adds to Europe's ineffectiveness at 'accounting for foreign purchases of European public debt'. The authors suggest that the EU should correctly record these foreign purchases, as it is the case in Japan or in the US.[19] Finally, according to estimates made in 2011, China holds a quarter of its official reserves in Euro.

For Eichengreen (2011b), the solution partly lies in the creation of a facility financed by the G20 in particular by Asian countries, which are 'flush with funds', and would purchase preferred shares in European banks. He further suggests that, on the model of the Brady bonds offered to Latin American countries at the end of the 1980s, the IMF could 'offer credit enhancements on the new bonds by creating a facility to underwrite a standby letter of credit'.[20]

Preserving the Euro has become a priority for China, which explains the fact that despite the sovereign debt crisis the Euro has not lost much of its value: the Chinese central bank and the State Administration of Foreign Exchange (SAFE), the most important Chinese Sovereign Wealth Fund,

19 'The scramble for Europe', July 2011.

20 'It is time for outsiders to save the single currency', *Financial Times*, 6 September 2011.

have bought huge quantities of Euro in order to diversify their official reserves away from the dollar, as Japan did. 'China does not want to be exposed to a chronically weak European currency when its own exports are being hit by inflation at home and by the threat of protectionism in some of its main markets, led by the United States' (Marsh 2011). In addition, as a counterpart for its interventions as a buyer of several Euro area members' public debt, China has asked the EU to recognise its market economy status, which according to the agreement made in 2001 when China joined the World Trade Organisation, should normally intervene in 2016. This status would lead to lifting of restrictions concerning Chinese investments in the EU and exports to the EU; moreover it would be more difficult for Western countries to use the WTO international settlement body in antidumping procedures against Chinese firms.[21]

Future development of the debt crisis

Finally, we shall analyse different scenarios of future development of the debt crisis, as well as pros and cons of exiting the Euro area. If a country were to exit the Euro area, what would be the consequences, for the country itself and for the Euro area? For the country, it would mean reintroducing a currency and issuing new notes and coins; the currency would quickly lose its value, due to the capital outflows that the country would face and because the central bank would be likely to ease monetary policy in order for the country to gain a competitive advantage on the world markets and improve growth prospects. Exports may thus be encouraged but imports would become very costly and the inflation rate would increase; the debt would become a bigger burden since it would be more difficult for the country to service the debt originally issued in Euro (even if inflation tends to decrease the burden of real public debt); this would ultimately cause a

21 Rinaldi-Larribe, Lightfoot, Zhao (2009).

partial default of the country, making it more difficult for the country to issue new debt on the financial market, due of a loss in confidence. Benefits may very rapidly prove to be lower than costs for a country which would leave the EMU. The economic and political costs of an exit from the Euro area are thus very high. The benefits are far from being as important: a devalued currency would undoubtedly make the exports of the country cheaper on the world markets, but the transitory gain would certainly not outweigh the costs incurred if the country abandons the Euro. In political terms, it would have severe consequences on the country's relations with other European countries.

From a legal aspect, the Treaty on the European Union includes no provision about the prospect of a country leaving the Euro area; but the consolidated version of the Treaty on the European Union mentions in Art. 50 (2) that a Member State may decide to withdraw from the Union (as a whole, not from the Euro area only) 'in accordance with its own constitutional requirements. A Member State which decides to withdraw shall notify the European Council of its intention. In the light of the guidelines provided by the European Council, the Union shall negotiate and conclude an agreement with that State, setting out the arrangements for its withdrawal, taking account of the framework for its future relationship with the Union.'[22]

For Artus (2011), if Greece were to leave the Euro area, it would experience a long recession (of at least 18 months) with a decrease in the purchasing power due to inflation as a consequence of the devaluation (with an increase in the price of imports of around 30%) and resulting from the monetisation of public debt as long as the current account deficit lasts. Besides, the economist states that if one takes into consideration the levels of sovereign debt, public deficit and external deficit of Greece, the country would have to devalue its currency by 55% in order to restore the balance.[23] Artus believes that Greece should be given six years instead of three to cut its deficit, in order for the country to be able to restore growth and com-

22 Official Journal of the European Union C 83/43, EN 30.3.2010.

23 *Le Figaro*, 13 September 2011.

petitiveness. Similarly, for Union des Banques Suisses (in 2011) the cost of leaving the Euro area for Greece would amount to 9500 to 11.500 Euro per person the first year, which represents 40 to 50% of its GDP. The following years, the cost would fall to 3.000 to 4.000 Euro per year.[24]

The Economist Intelligence Unit had designed three possible scenarios in 2011: the first one, presented at the time as the most likely one (50% probability), considered that peripheral countries of the Euro area are able to cut their deficits, restore their competitiveness and that 'creditor countries provide enough financial support to contain the crisis until orderly restructuring of some sovereign debt is carried out in 2013'. The second scenario (25% probability) entitled 'main risk scenario' was less optimistic and assumed that the austerity plans were uneasy to maintain and that creditors and markets would lose faith in the ability of peripheral countries to meet their engagements; in this scenario the Euro zone would hold together 'but in poor shape'. The third scenario was of course even less optimistic but the EIU believed it would be likely to occur with a 15% probability only (the 'ultimate risk scenario'); this scenario considered that weak countries might have to leave the Euro area, and that Germany itself might be tempted to exit the EMU, although it has benefited greatly from it, through an easy access to markets. The last scenario was entitled the 'golden one' since the Euro area emerged 'strengthened from the crisis'. Of course this analysis has been carried out two years ago, and it would be interesting to see whether forecasts look much different today. As time passes, although Greece is still in the Euro area as at the end of 2013, it seems like the economic situation of the country has not improved, despite the two bailout packages put in place in May 2010 and July 2011 by Euro area countries, bilaterally or through the European Financial Stability Facility, and by the IMF. An agreement has been found between Eurozone countries, on 27 October 2011, according to which 50% of the debt owed by the country to private banks (100 billion Euro) would be written-off. The agreement was welcomed by the markets, but the Greek Prime Minister decided, a few days later, to hold a referendum on the subject, before changing his

24 *Les Echos*, 13 September 2011.

mind again, and before he finally had to walk out. Moreover the scenarios do not take into account the Cyprus episode of the Eurozone crisis, which will not be developed here. Are we facing a situation that has worsened today, compared to 2011, or on the contrary is it getting better owing to the reforms that have been undertaken? The resignation of the chief economist of the ECB, Jürgen Stark, in September 2011, was another worrying sign for the markets, since it signalled the existence of tensions between key ECB members; it could also be interpreted as the illustration of the division among German personalities on the ECB policy, notably concerning the purchase of debt instruments from peripheral countries.[25]

The good news at mid-2013 seems to be the renewed growth in the Eurozone, in the second quarter of the year, since real GDP has expanded by 0.3% compared to the previous quarter, even if in annual terms GDP is still expected to contract by 0.7%. Many countries are still in recession nevertheless.[26] In 2012, the Euro area was in recession for the first time (-0.6%), with only seven countries on a slightly positive trend. In the EU, the pattern is more or less the same with a recession in 2012 (-0.3%) and an expected -0.1% in 2013. Concerning the evolution of public finances, in 2012 the budget deficit of the Euro area represented 3.7% of GDP, which was lower than in the US (8.9%) or than in the UK (6.3% of GDP); in terms of public debt also, the Euro area stands at 90.6% in 2012 whereas the public debt of the US has reached 109.8% of GDP, and the British one lies at 90% of GDP. As to the EU27 average, it stands at 4% for the public deficit and 85.3% for the public debt, in 2012. Except for Greece (which represents 0.3% of the Euro area GDP), Ireland, Spain and Portugal, the situation in other Euro area countries seems to be under control, even though Italy and Spain may continue to encounter some difficulties to finance their debt. Nevertheless a break-up of the Euro area seems unlikely due to political efforts put into the creation of the single currency, and due to the economic benefits that members have drawn from the Euro, despite the costs. Moreover Ireland

25 On 13 September 2011, the ECB had already bought 35 billion Euro of Spanish and Italian bonds, and 76 billion Euro of Greek, Irish and Portuguese bonds.

26 The Economist Intelligence Unit (2013) 'Euro zone exits recession in Q2', 14 August.

has been able to renew with growth after a very harsh recession following the implementation of painful austerity measures; unit labour costs have fallen since private and public sector wages have decreased (after 2008), and the retirement age has increased. Exports have grown, leading to a sharp improvement in the current account balance in 2011. Spain has also made huge efforts to tackle the issue of ailing banks; the unemployment rate is still very high but the country should see its exports grow by 4.1% in 2013, according to the European Commission. Structural reforms have been undertaken on the labour market, to increase flexibility, leading to wage moderation; as a consequence the country's exports have become more competitive, and the current account deficit has narrowed down from almost 10% of GDP in 2007 to 1% in 2012.[27] For 2013, it should be positive, as shown in Table 3. Portugal and Greece have also experienced an increase in their exports, owing to a decline in their ULC.

For Marsh (2011), 'whatever the setbacks it faced and the strains it may continue to suffer, the Euro is most unlikely to collapse and disappear. In the intricate work on assembling common European money, too great was the expenditure of political and economic capital, too arduous were the efforts of many governments from many nations over many years, for the product of their labours simply to wither and die'.

Conclusion

As P. De Grauwe (2006) has argued, 'the European monetary union is a remarkable achievement. Yet it also remains fragile because of a flaw in its governance'. This flaw is linked to the non-existence of a European government with the power to spend and to tax, which would be independent from national governments, which entails the absence of a minimal degree

27 'Spain's exporting prowess brightens economic gloom', Buck T., *Financial Times*, 9 May 2013.

of budgetary integration and of political unification. The author states that 'these flaws will have to be fixed, but that it will be difficult to do so, because of a general "integration fatigue"', and that 'at least it should be told that failure to do so implies that the European monetary union has no future'. When we see what the crisis has produced these last few years, we realise that it is very unfortunate that P. De Grauwe's advice in 2006 has not been followed.

Currently we are not experiencing a crisis of the Euro but a crisis of the sovereign debt of certain member states. The creation of Eurobonds is a real necessity if we want to avoid a further spreading of the debt crisis to other bigger countries; the sake of the Euro is contingent to the acceptance of the existence of these Eurobonds by reluctant countries such as Germany, Finland, Austria, the Netherlands and Slovakia. Reforms have been made that were absolutely essential in order to reinforce the supervision and the surveillance in the Euro area as we have seen; but countries now need to agree on a reform of the European budget, so as to increase its size: a budget that merely represents 1% of the total GDP of the EU members does not serve its purpose even though many policies remain in the hands of the different governments. Economic governance will really be efficient if accompanied by a decent budget and by a representative of the Eurozone (a sort of 'finance minister') who intervenes on behalf of the members, and who embodies the Eurozone at the IMF for example. In substance, we must move towards more federalism, less intergovernmentalism. Crises will be solved more rapidly, in less panic and with fewer hesitations. Moreover, many of the Euro area countries should implement the structural reforms needed to allow the Euro area to come closer to an Optimum Currency Area: flexibility of labour, product and services markets, integration of financial markets, and of course for many countries a real public finance reform. Economic policy coordination must be enhanced, and an early warning system must enable authorities and European institutions to detect anomalies early enough for imbalances and bubbles to be corrected before they get out of control.

Martin Wolf wrote in the *Financial Times*, on 8 March 2011: 'While many Germans are angry over the sloppy behaviour of certain partners, the country's elite remains aware of both the perils of isolation and the benefits of the stability that the European project has brought to their country in its relations with all its neighbours'. Still some form of break-up remains conceivable if the politicians and the population consider that membership is incompatible with monetary stability. Wolf argues that 'the Eurozone is highly likely to survive' because it is 'backed by a profound political commitment', because of the long-term interests of members who can afford it, and because 'the Eurozone has the will and the wherewithal to keep the Euro experiment afloat'. This opinion is of course shared by the former President of the ECB, J-C. Trichet (2009) for whom the Euro has improved price transparency, increased trade and promoted economic and financial integration, not only within the Euro area but globally; the financial crisis has shown that 'in turbulent financial waters, it is better to be on a large, solid and steady ship than on a small vessel. Would Europe have been able to act as swiftly, decisively and coherently if we had not had the single currency uniting us? Would we have been able to protect many separate national currencies from the fallout of the financial crisis?' This viewpoint is confirmed by many authors, according to whom the Euro has limited the impact of the financial crisis in the area, since it has prevented the turbulences associated with exchange rate and interest rate shocks that member states had experienced in the past, especially during the 1992–3 crisis.

Nevertheless, the Euro area should continue reforming its governance rules, increasing the coordination of economic policies and going towards a closer political union; it should boost financial integration and market supervision, improve its growth perspectives by putting the accent on innovation and market flexibility and by completing the Single Market in the services area, and of course by restoring its public finances. This is a huge task, but compared to the progress that has been accomplished since the Treaty of Rome, the end goals seem within reach.

In the short to medium term, what is needed is a sustainable growth rate in Euro area countries, as well as a pledge to structural reforms and sound macroeconomic policies; external and internal imbalances such as current account imbalances and excessive private and/or public debt must be closely monitored and combated; flexibility of the labour and product markets needs to be enhanced and the single market must be achieved and innovation encouraged, for economic growth to be stronger. The problem is that austerity measures are necessary for markets and investors to regain confidence but at the same time they do not provide the appropriate environment that would encourage growth, making it difficult to achieve the goals in terms of reduction in the public deficit and public debt.

Tsoukalis (2011) has given a strong message of hope in the Journal of Common Market Studies Annual Review lecture, with which I shall conclude this chapter: 'crisis is the mother of change, and crises in the past have often provided the catalyst for further integration in Europe'.

References

Aguiar-Conraria, L. and Soares, M. J. (2011) 'Business cycle synchronisation across the Euro area: a wavelet analysis', *Journal of Macroeconomics*, Vol. 33, Issue 3, September, pp. 477–89.

Altavilla, C. (2004) 'Do EMU Members share the same business cycle?', *Journal of Common Market Studies*, Vol. 42, No. 5, pp. 869–96.

Amato, G., Verhofstadt, G. (2011), 'A plan to save the Euro and curb the speculators', *Financial Times*, 4 July.

Angeloni, I., Bénassy-Quéré, A., Carton, B., Darvas, Z., Destais, C., Pisani-Ferry, J., Sapir, A., Vallée, S. (2011) 'Global currencies for tomorrow: a European perspective', Bruegel Blueprint 13, CEPII Research Report 2011–01.

Artis, M. (2003) 'Is there a European business cycle?', CESifo Working Paper No. 1053.

Artus, P. (2011), *Le Figaro*, 13 September.

Babetskii, I. (2004) 'EU enlargement and endogeneity of some OCA criteria: evidence from the CEECs', Czech National Bank Working Paper Series 2/2004.

Berger, H. and Nitsch, V. (2006) 'Zooming out: the trade effect of the Euro in historical perspective', CESifo Workshop on Euro-Area Enlargement, Conference Paper, 24 November 2006, Munich.

Bower, U. and Guillemineau, C. (2006) 'Determinants of business cycle synchronisation across Euro area countries', European Central Bank Working Paper Series, No. 587, February.

Buck, T. (2013), 'Spain's exporting prowess brightens economic gloom', *Financial Times*, 9 May.

Darvas, Z. and Szapary, G. (2004) 'Business cycle synchronisation in the enlarged EU: comovements in the new and old members', Magyar Nemzeti Bank Working Paper, 2004/1.

Darvas, Z., Rose, A. K. and Szapary, G. (2005) 'Fiscal divergence and business cycle synchronisation: irresponsibility is idiosyncratic', MNB Working Paper, 2005/3.

De Grauwe, P. (1997) *The economics of monetary integration*, Oxford, Oxford University Press.

De Grauwe, P. (2006) 'What have we learnt about monetary integration since the Maastricht Treaty?', *Journal of Common Market Studies*, Vol. 44, No. 4, pp. 711–30.

De Grauwe, P. (2008) 'The Euro at ten: achievements and challenges', Chapter presented as the keynote lecture at the Annual meeting of the Austrian Economic Association in Vienna, 23 May 2008.

De Haan, J., Inklaar, R. and Jong-a-Pin, R. (2005) 'Will business cycles in the Euro area converge? A critical survey of empirical research', CCSO Centre for Economic Research, University of Groningen, Working Paper 2005/08.

Deutsche Bank Research, Basten, C. (2006) 'Business cycle synchronisation in the Euro area: Development, determinants and implications', Working paper series, Research notes 22, 11 October.

Dijsselbloem, J. (2013) 'Ministers put straitjacket on bailout fund', Euractiv.com, 21 June.

The Economist Intelligence Unit (2011) 'State of the Union: can the Euro zone survive its debt crisis?', Special report, March.

The Economist Intelligence Unit (2013) 'Euro zone exits recession in Q2', 14 August.

Eichengreen, B. (2011a) 'Le dollar n'est pas près de perdre sa place', *Telos*, 11 January.

Eichengreen, B. (2011b) 'It is time for outsiders to save the single currency', *Financial Times*, 6 September.

European Central Bank (2004) 'The acceding countries' strategies towards ERM II and the adoption of the Euro: an analytical review', *Occasional Paper Series*, No. 10.

European Central Bank (2013) 'The International Role of the Euro', July.

European Council on Foreign Relations (2011) 'The scramble for Europe', July.

Fields, D. and Vernengo, M. (2011) 'Hegemonic Currencies during the Crisis: The Dollar versus the Euro in a Cartalist Perspective', Working Paper No. 666, Levy Economics Institute of Bard College, April.

Firdnuc, J. and Korhonen, I. (2001) 'Similarity of supply and demand shocks between the Euro area and the CEECs', Bank of Finland Institute for Economies in Transition BOFIT Discussion Papers, No. 14.

Frankel, J. and Chinn, M. (2005) 'Will the Euro Eventually Surpass the Dollar as Leading International Reserve Currency?', NBER Working Paper, No. 11510, August.

Frankel, J. and Rose, A. (1998) 'The endogeneity of the O. C. A. criteria', *Economic Journal*, No. 108, pp. 1009–25.

Gayer, C. (2007) 'A fresh look at business cycle synchronisation in the Euro area', European Economy, Economic Papers, Directorate-General for Economic and Financial Affairs, European Commission, No. 287, September.

Goulard, S. (2011), 'Qui parle au nom de l'Euro ?' Les Echos, 29 June.

Hankel, W., Nölling, W. and Schachtschneider, K. A. (2010) 'A Euro exit is the only way out for Greece', *Financial Times*, 25 March.

Ifo Institute (2011) 'What will Eurobonds cost?' 17 August.

Kenen, P. (1969) 'The theory of optimum currency areas: an eclectic view', in Mundell, R. and Swoboda, A. (eds), *Monetary problems of the international economy*, Chicago, University of Chicago Press.

Krugman, P. (2003) 'Lessons of Massachusetts for EMU' In F. Torres and Giavazzi, F. (eds), *Adjustment and growth in the European Monetary Union*, Cambridge, Cambridge University Press.

Lane, P. (2006) 'The real effects of EMU', American Economic Association AEA 2006 Conference paper, January.

Lemoine, M. (2011) 'L'Euro a un avenir', Fondation Robert Schuman Policy Paper, Question d'Europe, No. 201, 11 April.

Mac Kinnon, R. (1963) 'Optimal currency areas', *American Economic Review*, Vol. 53, pp. 717–24.

Marsh, D. (2011) 'Faltering ambitions and unrequited hopes: the battle for the Euro intensifies', *Journal of Common Market Studies*, Vol. 49, Annual Review, pp. 45–55.

Micco, A., Stein, E. and Ordonez, G. (2003) 'The currency union effect on trade: early evidence from EMU', *Economic Policy*, October, pp. 315–56.

Mink, M., Jacobs, J. and De Haan, J. (2007), 'Measuring synchronicity and co-movement of business cycles with an application to the Euro area', *CESifo Working Paper*, No. 2112, October.

Mundell, R. (1961) 'A theory of optimal currency areas', *American Economic Review*, Vol. 51, pp. 657–65.

Mundell, R. (1997) 'A theory of optimum currency areas', in Blejer, M. I., Frenkel, J. A., Leiderman L. and Rozin A. (eds), *Optimum currency areas – New analytical and policy developments*, International Monetary Fund.

Official Journal of the European Union C 83/43, EN 30.3.2010. <http://eur-lex.Europa.eu/LexUriServ/LexUriServ.do?uri=OJ:C:2010:083:0013:0046:EN:PDF>.

Pisani-Ferry, J. and Sapir, A. (2009) 'Weathering the storm', Bruegel Policy Contribution, 2009/3, April.

Prandi, M. (2011) 'Sortie de l'euro: le scenario catastrophe', *Les Echos*, 13 September.

Regling, K., Deroose, S., Felke, R. and Kutos, P. (2010) 'The Euro after the first decade: weathering the financial storm and enlarging the Euro area', Asian Development Bank Institute, Working Paper Series, No. 205, March.

Rinaldi-Larribe, M.-J., Lightfoot, W. S., and Zhao, Z. (2009) 'Does China deserve the market economy status?', *Journal of Chinese Economic and Foreign Trade Studies*, Vol. 2, No. 2, pp. 110–20.

Rose, A. (2000) 'One money, one market: estimating the effect of common currencies on trade', *Economic Policy*, 30, pp. 7–46.

Trichet, J.-C. (2009) Exclusive interview from the Fondation Robert Schuman, 18 March 2009.

Tsoukalis, L. (2011) 'The JCMS Annual Review Lecture: The shattering of illusions – And what next?', *Journal of Common Market Studies*, Vol. 49, Annual Review, pp. 19–44.

Van De Coevering, C. (2003) 'Structural convergence and monetary integration in Europe', De Nederlandsche Bank MEB Series, No. 2003–20.

Wolf, M. (2011) 'Why the Eurozone will survive', *Financial Times*, 8 March 2011.

Zentrum für Europäische Wirtschaftsforschung, ZEW (2008), Bureau of European Policy Advisers, Project for the European Commission, BEPA-01/2007-PO, Mannheim and Vienna, November.

Appendix

Table 1: Evolution of public deficits and public debts in Euro area and non-Euro area countries

	2006		*2007*		*2008*		*2009*		*2010*		*2011*		*2012*	
Euro area countries	Public Def.	Public debt	Public Def.	Public debt	Public Def.	Public debt	Public Def.	Public debt	Public Def.	Public debt	Public Def.	Public debt	Public Def.	Public debt
Germany	-1.6	67.6	0.3	64.9	0.1	66.3	-3.1	74.5	-4.1	82.4	-0.8	80.4	0.2	81.9
Neth.	0.5	47.9	0.2	45.3	0.6	58.2	-5.6	60.8	-5.1	63.1	-4.5	65.5	-4.1	71.2
Belgium	0.3	88.2	-0.4	84.2	-1.4	89.6	-5.6	95.7	-3.8	95.5	-3.7	97.8	-3.9	99.6
Lux.	1.3	6.6	3.6	6.7	3.0	13.6	-0.8	15.3	-0.9	19.2	-0.2	18.3	-0.8	20.8
Austria	-1.5	61.8	-0.4	60.7	-0.9	63.8	-4.1	69.2	-4.5	72.0	-2.5	72.5	-2.5	73.4
Finland	4.1	39.2	5.2	35.2	4.2	34.1	-2.5	43.5	-2.5	48.6	-0.8	49.0	-1.9	53.0
France	-2.4	63.6	-2.7	63.9	-3.3	67.7	-7.5	79.2	-7.1	82.4	-5.3	85.8	-4.8	90.2
Italy	-3.4	106.5	-1.5	103.6	-2.7	106.3	-5.5	116.4	-4.5	119.3	-3.8	120.8	-3.0	127.0
Spain	1.8	39.7	1.9	36.1	-4.2	39.8	-11.2	53.9	-9.7	61.5	-9.4	69.3	-10.6	84.2
Portugal	-3.9	64.7	-2.8	68.3	-3.0	71.6	-10.2	83.7	-9.8	94.0	-4.4	108.3	-6.4	123.6
Ireland	3.0	25.1	0.0	25.0	-7.3	44.4	-13.9	64.8	-30.8	96.1	-13.4	106.4	-7.6	117.6
Greece	-2.6**	95.3**	-6.4	105.4	-9.4	110.7	-15.6	129.7	-10.7	148.3	-9.5	170.3	-10.0	156.9
Slovenia	-1.2	27.2	0.0	23.1	-1.8	21.9	-6.2	35.0	-5.9	38.6	-6.4	46.9	-4.0	54.1
Cyprus	-1.2	64.8	3.4	58.3	0.9	48.3	-6.1	58.5	-5.3	61.3	-6.3	71.1	-6.3	85.8
Malta	-2.5	64.2	-2.2	62.0	-4.5	61.5	-3.7	66.4	-3.6	67.4	-2.8	70.3	-3.3	72.1
Slovakia	-3.6*	30.4	-1.9	29.6	-2.1	27.8	-8.0	35.6	-7.7	41.0	-5.1	43.3	-4.3	52.1
Estonia	3.4*	4.2	2.6*	3.7	-2.8	4.6	-2.0	7.2	0.2	6.7	1.2	6.2	-0.3	10.1
EA average	*-1.3***	*68.5***	*-0.6*	*66.3*	*-2.0*	*70.0*	*-6.4*	*80.0*	*-6.2*	*85.4*	*-4.2*	*87.3*	*-3.7*	*90.6*
	2006		*2007*		*2008*		*2009*		*2010*		*2011*		*2012*	
Non-Euro area countries	Pub Def.	Public debt	Public Def.	Public debt	Public Def.	Public debt	Public Def.	Public debt	Public Def.	Public debt	Public Def.	Public debt	Public Def.	Public debt
UK	-2.6	43.1	-2.8	44.5	-5.0	54.4	-11.5	67.8	-10.2	79.4	-7.8	85.5	-6.3	90.0
Denmark	4.8	30.4	4.8	27.5	3.2	34.5	-2.7	40.7	-2.5	42.7	-1.8	46.4	-4.0	45.8
Sweden	2.3	45.9	3.8	40.2	2.2	38.8	-0.7	42.6	0.3	39.4	0.2	38.4	-0.5	38.2
Poland	-3.8	47.6	-1.9	45.0	-3.7	47.1	-7.4	50.9	-7.9	54.8	-5.0	56.2	-3.9	55.6
Hungary	-9.2	65.6	-5.0	66.1	-3.7	72.3	-4.6	79.8	-4.3	81.8	4.3	81.4	-1.9	79.2
Czech Rep.	-2.7	29.4	-0.7	29.0	-2.7	30.0	-5.8	34.2	-4.8	37.8	-3.3	40.8	-4.4	45.8
Latvia	-0.2	10.7	-0.3	9.0	-4.2	19.7	-9.8	36.9	-8.1	44.4	-3.6	41.9	-1.2	40.7

Lithuania	-0.5	18.2	-1.0	16.9	-3.3	15.6	-9.4	29.3	-7.2	37.9	-5.5	38.5	-3.2	40.7
Romania	-2.2	12.4	-2.5	12.6	-5.7	13.4	-9.0	23.6	-6.8	30.5	-5.6	34.7	-2.9	37.8
Bulgaria	3.0	22.7	0.1	17.2	1.7	13.7	-4.3	14.6	-3.1	16.2	-2.0	16.3	-0.8	18.5
EU27 average	*-1.4***	*61.3***	*-0.8*	*59.0*	*-2.4*	*62.3*	*-6.9*	*74.6*	*-6.5*	*80.0*	*-4.4*	*82.5*	*-4.0*	*85.3*

* not in the Euro area at that time

** underestimated because of Greek cheating

Source: EIU 2011, European Commission 2008, 2009, 2010, 2011, Eurostat 2013.

Table 2: Evolution of several economic indicators in Euro area and non-Euro area countries

	Growth rates						*Inflation rates*					
	1997–2001	*2002–6*	*2008*	*2011*	*2012*	*2013^e*	*1997–2001*	*2002–6*	*2008*	*2011*	*2012*	*2013^e*
Euro area countries												
Germany	2.1	1.0	1.1	2.6	0.7	0.4	1.2	1.6	2.8	2.5	2.1	1.8
Netherlands	3.7	1.6	1.9	1.0	-1.0	-0.8	2.6	2.1	2.2	2.5	2.8	2.8
Belgium	2.7	2.0	1.0	1.8	-0.3	0.0	1.7	2.0	4.5	3.4	2.6	1.3
Luxembourg	6.3	4.1	1.4	1.7	0.3	0.8	1.9	2.9	4.1	3.7	2.9	1.9
Austria	2.6	2.2	2.2	2.7	0.8	0.6	1.3	1.7	3.2	3.6	2.6	2.0
Finland	4.5	3.0	0.9	2.8	-0.2	0.3	1.9	1.1	3.9	3.3	3.2	2.4
France	3.0	1.7	0.2	2.0	0.0	-0.1	1.2	2.1	3.2	2.3	2.2	1.2
Italy	2.0	0.9	-1.3	0.4	-2.4	-1.3	2.1	2.4	3.5	2.9	3.3	1.6
Spain	4.4	3.3	0.9	0.4	-1.4	-1.5	2.4	3.3	4.1	3.1	2.4	1.5
Portugal	3.9	0.7	0.0	-1.6	-3.2	-2.3	2.7	2.9	2.7	3.6	2.8	0.7
Ireland	9.2	5.4	-3.5	1.4	0.9	1.1	3.0	3.2	3.1	1.2	1.9	1.3
Greece	3.8	4.2	1.0	-7.1	-6.4	-4.2	3.7	3.4	4.2	3.1	1.0	-0.8
Slovenia	4.2	4.3	3.7	0.6	-2.3	-2.0	8.0	4.3	5.5	2.1	2.8	2.2
Cyprus	4.2	3.3	3.6	0.5	-2.4	-8.7	2.7	2.6	4.4	3.5	3.1	1.0
Malta	3.4	2.0	5.3	1.8	1.0	1.4	3.1	2.5	4.7	2.5	3.2	1.9
Slovakia	2.7	5.9	5.8	3.2	2.0	1.0	8.5	5.3	3.9	4.1	3.7	1.9
Estonia	7.0	8.5	-5.1	8.3	3.2	3.0	6.1	3.3	10.6	5.1	4.2	3.6
EA av.	2.8	1.7	0.4	1.5	-0.6	-0.4	1.8	2.2	3.3	2.7	2.5	1.6
Non-Euro area countries												
UK	3.4	2.6	-0.1	1.0	0.3	0.6	1.3	1.7	3.6	4.5	2.8	2.8
Denmark	2.4	1.8	-1.1	1.1	-0.5	0.7	2.1	1.8	3.6	2.7	2.4	1.1
Sweden	3.4	3.3	-0.6	3.7	0.7	1.5	1.5	1.5	3.3	1.4	0.9	0.9
Poland	4.4	4.1	5.1	4.5	1.9	1.1	9.8	1.9	4.2	3.9	3.7	1.4
Hungary	4.3	3.9	0.8	1.6	-1.7	0.2	12.3	4.8	6.0	3.9	5.7	2.6
Czech Rep.	1.2	4.6	2.5	1.9	-1.3	-0.4	5.6	1.5	6.3	2.1	3.5	1.9
Latvia	6.3	9.0	-4.2	5.5	5.6	3.8	3.9	4.9	15.3	4.2	2.3	1.4
Lithuania	4.7	8.0	2.9	5.9	3.7	3.1	3.9	1.4	11.1	4.1	3.2	2.1

Romania	0.1	6.2	7.3	2.2	0.7	1.6	63.2	12.9	7.9	5.8	3.4	4.3
Bulgaria	2.5	6.0	6.2	1.8	0.8	0.9	n.a.	5.5	12.0	3.4	2.4	2.0
EU 27	2.9	2.1	0.5	1.6	-0.3	-0.1	4.3	2.3	3.7	3.1	2.6	1.8
United States	3.8	2.7	0.0	1.8	2.2	1.9	2.5	2.6	3.8	3.2	2.1	1.8
Japan	0.5	1.7	-1.2	-0.6	2.0	1.4	0.1	-0.2	1.4	-0.3	0.0	0.2

Source: EIU 2011, European Commission 2008, 2009, 2010, 2011, Eurostat 2013.

Table 3: Average current account balances in OECD countries 1997–2013

	CA balance					
	1997–2001	*2002–6*	*2008*	*2011*	*2012^e^*	*2013^e^*
Euro area countries						
Germany	-0.8	4.2	6.7	5.6	6.4	6.3
Netherlands	4.8	7.5	4.8	8.3	8.2	8.6
Belgium	4.5	4.5	1.1	1.0	0.9	1.4
Luxembourg	10.0	10.5	5.3	7.1	5.6	6.3
Austria	-1.4	2.4	3.7	2.1	3.0	3.1
Finland	6.4	5.6	2.9	-1.3	-1.6	-1.7
France	1.9	-0.6	-2.7	-2.6	-1.8	-1.6
Italy	1.2	-1.0	-3.2	-3.1	-0.5	1.0
Spain	-2.4	-6.0	-9.6	-3.7	-0.9	1.6
Portugal	-8.8	-8.9	-12.6	-7.2	-1.9	0.1
Ireland	0.5	-1.3	-5.6	1.1	5.0	3.1
Greece	-6.7	-11.8	-9.6	-11.7	-5.3	-2.8
Slovenia	-1.8	-1.4	-6.8	0.1	2.7	4.8
Cyprus	-1.3	-5.0	-17.0	-4.8	-4.8	-1.9
Malta	-6.4	-4.9	-5.6	-0.5	-0.8	0.0
Slovakia	-6.5	-7.5	-6.9	-2.5	2.0	2.5
Estonia	-7.4	-11.8	-8.8	0.6	-3.1	-2.2
EA av.	0.4	0.5	-0.8	0.1	1.2	1.9
Non-Euro area countries						
UK	-1.5	-2.3	-1.6	-1.3	-3.7	-2.7
Denmark	1.2	3.3	2.7	5.6	5.2	4.5
Sweden	4.7	6.7	8.9	7.3	7.0	7.0
Poland	-4.0	-2.4	-4.8	-4.5	-3.3	-2.5

Hungary	-6.2	-8.1	-6.9	1.0	1.9	2.5
Czech Rep.	-4.1	-4.4	-0.8	-3.9	-2.6	-2.4
Latvia	-7.3	-12.5	-13.1	-2.4	-1.7	-2.1
Lithuania	-8.5	-7.4	-13.1	-3.7	-0.5	-1.0
Romania	-5.4	-6.3	-11.4	-4.5	-4.0	-3.9
Bulgaria	-2.3	-8.7	-23.2	0.1	-1.1	-2.6
EU 27	0.0	0.0	-1.0	-0.2	0.5	1.2
United States	-3.0	-5.2	-4.7	-3.3	-3.0	-2.8
Japan	2.5	3.5	3.2	2.0	1.1	1.8

Source: European Commission Spring 2011 & Spring 2013, Coface 2011.

Table 4: Share of the US dollar and of the Euro in global markets (in percentage)

	US dollar						Euro					
	2001	2008	2009	2010	2011	2012	2001	2008	2009	2010	2011	2012
Currency shares in foreign exchange reserves (at current exchange rates)	71.5	64.1	62.0	61.8	62.3	61.9	19.2	26.4	27.7	26.0	24.7	23.9
In advanced economies	70.6	67.2	65.2	64.2	66.3	63.5	19.0	23.1	25.3	24.6	22.9	23.7
In emerging and developing economies	73.8	60.7	58.5	58.3	57.6	60.1	19.7	30.0	30.2	28.3	27.4	24.2
FX turnover (out of 200%)	90.3 (1999)	85.6	84.9	80.0	87.4	86.0	37.6 (1999)	n.a.	39.1	39.1	45.2	41.2
Stock of international debt securities (at current exchange rates)	50.5	44.5	45.6	48.5	50.8	52.4	23.1	32.4	31.7	27.8	25.8	25.5
Denomination of trade with non-Euro-area countries												
Euro-area exports							45.4	63.6	64.1	63.6	64.9	62.5
Euro-area imports							44.4	47.5	45.2	49.5	49.8	49.0

Source: Bruegel 2011, ECB 2013, IMF 2013, Bank of England 2011 and 2013.

Table 5: Share of the Japanese yen and other currencies (except Pound sterling and Swiss Franc) in global markets (in percentage)

	Yen						Other currencies					
	2001	2008	2009	2010	2011	2012	2001	2008	2009	2010	2011	2012
Global holdings of foreign exchange reserves current ER	5	3.1	2.9	3.8	3.5	3.9	1.3	2.2	3.0	4.4	5.4	6.1
In advanced economies	6.1	4.3	3.9	4.7	4.2	4.7	1.4	2.5	2.6	3.9	3.9	5.0
In emerging and developing economies	2.4	1.9	1.8	2.8	2.7	3.0	1.0	1.9	3.5	5.0	6.9	7.4

Source: ECB 2011, IMF 2013.

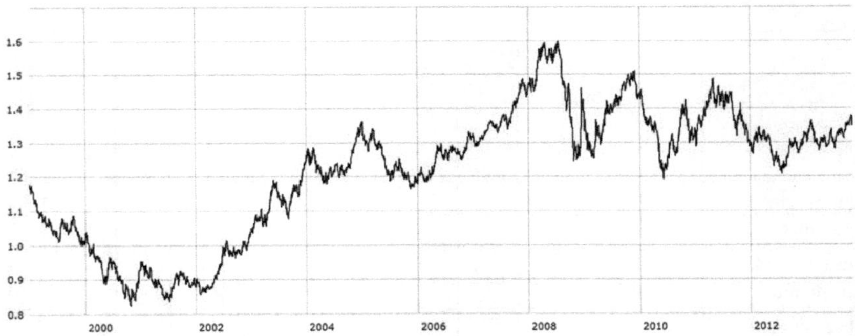

Source: ECB, October 2013.

Figure 1: Evolution of the exchange rate Euro/US dollar since January 1999.

JOHN RYAN

3 China and the Global Role of Currencies

This chapter will examine four scenarios regarding the global currency regime of the future and the Chinese influence in this most important policy arena. It will focus on the US Dollar as the dominant reserve currency, on the Euro as number two reserve currency, on the potential of the Renminbi to become a reserve currency, and on the IMF's Special Drawing Rights (SDRs).

Revisiting the Asian financial crisis of 1997

The Asian financial crisis began in 1997 when Thailand was forced to devalue its currency after it had exhausted its foreign currency reserves in an effort to defend its currency peg from speculators and investors keen to 'cash out'. The transition from a pegged currency to a free floating one caused the Thai Baht to lose half its value. The Thai Baht had been pegged at 25 Baht to the US Dollar and was devalued to 56 Baht to the US Dollar on 2 July 1997.

As investors' confidence collapsed throughout Asia, Indonesia, South Korea, the Philippines and Malaysia were all affected and their currencies devalued significantly.[1] Many factors were cited as causes to the Asian

1 Milne, A. (2009), *The fall of the House of Credit: What Went Wrong in Banking and What can be Done to Repair the Damage?* Cambridge, Cambridge University Press.

financial crisis.[2] Some commentators saw China's devaluation and subsequent export growth as one of the main causes.[3]

It is generally accepted that the increase in interest rates in the United States made the US Dollar more attractive to short-term investors. This led to an outflow of capital from the affected countries as international investors preferred US investments. This outflow, coupled with a slowdown in exports severely affected these economies' current account balance and led to devaluation. With local business and financial sector borrowing heavily denominated in US Dollars, devaluation and the lack of short-term capital (which had fled to the United States) led to a credit squeeze in the affected countries, which plunged many of them into recession. Other factors have also been highlighted as causes to the crisis, such as herd mentality by currency traders and speculation. Indeed Malaysian Prime Minister Mahathir Mohammed accused George Soros, a currency speculator, of ruining the Malaysian economy with extensive currency speculation. Soros was also implicated in Britain's 1992 exit from the Exchange Rate Mechanism of the European Monetary System, where he was alleged to have made £2 billion overnight speculating against the British Sterling.[4]

After the Asian Financial Crisis there was academic and political discourse[5] about the impact of a possible devaluation of the Renminbi and the negative global consequences that would be brought about should it be devalued.[6] An appreciation or floating of the Renminbi would have important consequences for growth and stability in China and knock-on

2 Blustein, P. (2001), *The Chastening: Inside the Crisis That Rocked the Global Financial System And Humbled the IMF.* New York, Public Affairs Books.

3 Weisbrot, M. August (2007), *Ten Years After: The Lasting Impact of the Asian Financial Crisis*, Center for Economic and Policy Research, London.

4 Fratianni, M. and Artis, M. J. (1996), 'The lira and the pound in the 1992 currency crisis: Fundamentals or speculation?' *Open Economics Review*, 7 (Supplement 1), 573–89.

5 Gang, F. (2006), 'Currency Asymmetry, Global Imbalances, and Rethinking of the International Currency System Global Imbalances and the US Debt Problem – Should Developing Countries Support the US Dollar?' Fondad, The Hague, December.

6 Liew, L. H. (2003), 'The Role of China's Bureaucracy in its No-Devaluation Policy during the Asian Financial Crisis'. *Japanese Journal of Political Science*, 4 (1), 61–76.

effects on the rest of Asia. Due to China's lack of sound financial and banking systems and the inherent structural problems China faced, a significant appreciation of the Renminbi, as Goldstein and Lardy[7] suggest, would lead to lower economic growth. The consequences on China's banking sector, due to its high amount of non-performing loans, would most likely lead to increasing deflationary pressures on an economy just emerging from deflation. Asset bubbles would most likely arise as well; foreign direct investment would drop, as investors flock to lower cost competitors.

The current debate on China's currency valuation and its effect on global trade imbalances can be seen as a distraction from the root causes of this imbalance. China's comparative advantage of cheap labour allows it a stronger hand when dealing with its trading partners, and the various fiscal policies implemented by its government make its exports much more competitive than any benefits an undervalued currency would confer. Since a sharp appreciation in the Renminbi would have dire consequences on the world economy, this would demonstrate the effect the Chinese currency has on the global financial market.

The Asian financial crisis of the late 1990s taught China and its neighbouring countries that it is better to have large amount of reserves as an insurance mechanism in front of the volatilities generated by the predatory and speculative capital flows inherent to the Dollar-dominated international monetary system based mostly on flexible exchange rates and free capital flows.[8] Secondly, this amount of reserves functions as a deterrent mechanism against diplomatic pressure coming out of Washington calling for the appreciation of the Chinese Renminbi. As the US Foreign Secretary Hillary Clinton admitted, it is not easy to be tough with your

7 Goldstein, M. and Lardy, N. (2008), 'Debating China's Exchange Rate Policy. Policy Analyses in International Economics'. Peterson Institute for International Economics, Washington D. C., April.

8 International Monetary Fund (IMF) (2010), 'Reserve Accumulation and International Monetary Stability', Strategy, Policy and Review Department, 13 April.

own banker.[9] The US has asked China to appreciate its currency in many different ways, but China has resisted the pressure, not least because it can always threaten to stop buying US debt. In this regard, China has increased its autonomy. It has been able to delay its adjustment costs for some time and it has avoided the pressure coming from the US.[10]

Scenario 1: The decline of the US Dollar as the global reserve currency

A significant portion of the Quantitative Easing (QE) package has sparked asset bubbles in high-return developing economies. This has prompted a tightening of capital controls. In addition, QE is US Dollar negative. As such, it only exacerbates so-called 'currency wars' – pushing the global economy all the closer to the slippery slope of competitive devaluations, trade frictions and protectionism.[11] Countless column inches were devoted to the supposed wickedness of China's currency policy. However, the biggest threat to the world economy comes from the US. Its policy mix (fiscally passive, monetarily aggressive) is ineffective.[12]

The US Dollar as the world's reserve currency makes the US a financial superpower. China's increased share in the International Monetary Fund (IMF) and its increased voting rights are a very big step forward for the internationalisation of the Renminbi. The problem is not that the value of this share is expressed in US Dollars, but that it would be best if the share

9 MacAskill, E. (2010), 'Wikileaks: Hillary Clinton's question: how can we stand up to Beijing', *The Guardian*, December 4.

10 Zhou, X. (2011), 'On Savings Ratio', *Financial Stability Review*, 15, Banque de France, February, 165–9.

11 Roach, S. (2010), 'Time to revamp the Fed's flawed mandate', *Financial Times*, 22 November.

12 Legrain, P. (2010), 'America's economic policy mix is a threat to the world', Voxeu.org, 2 November.

could be expressed in Renminbi. Therefore, for China to challenge the position of the US Dollar, it needs to take a path of internationalisation and directly confront the US Dollar. There are two options that China can consider. The first option is to sell US Dollar reserves. The second option is that China could slow down dramatically the purchases of US Dollars.[13]

There has been increasing pressure on China's officials to sell Chinese-held US Dollars and to create a de-Americanised world. This would include, as a key part of an effective reform, the introduction of a new international reserve currency that is to be created to replace the dominant US Dollar.[14]

China entered into a very large currency swap agreement with the Eurozone – this is considered a step toward establishing the Renminbi as a major world currency. This agreement will result in a reduction of US Dollars being used in trade between China and Europe. The swap deal will allow more trade and investment between the regions to be conducted in Euro and Renminbi, without having to convert into another currency such as the US Dollar. China currently owns about $1.3 trillion of US debt, and this enormous exposure to US debt is starting to become a major political issue among the country's leadership.[15]

The People's Bank of China (PBOC) has a large stock of US Dollars, and a pressing question is how it might diversify its assets. Increasing political tensions have given rise to fears that it might get rid of this huge bulk of securities and precipitate a US Dollar crash. In August 2007 a Chinese official indeed reminded the world that Beijing was in a position to provoke a 'mass depreciation' of the US Dollar if it decided to do so. China's authorities have so far shown few signs of attempting to weaken the US Dollar. China is the world's largest US Dollar investor, and no one else would have less interest in seeing the value of the US currency plummet.

13 Freeman, Kevin D. (2013), 'China Says That It's No Longer in Their Interest', 22 November, *Global Economic Warfare*.

14 Chang, Liu (2013), 'US fiscal failure warrants a de-Americanized world', Xinhua News Agency, 13 October.

15 'ECB to Create Currency Swap Line with China Central Bank', *Wall Street Journal*, 10 October 2013.

The soaring US debt now risks undermining the US Dollar and its enjoyment of its exorbitant privilege, while jeopardising the global economy at the same time. 'The Dollar may be our currency, but it's your problem', is a phrase that John Connolly, US Treasury Secretary under President Nixon, used to a delegation of European visitors in 1971. John Connolly's statement still has a ring of truth to it but the US Dollar is losing its status as the world's reserve currency. A reserve currency has to be stable to be effective, and for some time now, it has been clear that the US Dollar is losing the confidence of global markets.[16]

While money printing by the Federal Reserve on a trillion-Dollar scale may be new, currency wars are not. At best, currency wars lay open how countries steal growth from trading partners. At worst, they degenerate into inflation, recession, retaliation and possible violence as the scramble for resources leads to invasion and war. The historical precedents are sobering enough, but the dangers today are even greater, increased by the scale and complexity of financial linkages throughout the world.[17]

The Federal Reserve describes its policy of QE as a low interest rate policy in order to stimulate employment and economic growth. QE is the biggest redistribution of wealth from the middle class and the poor to the rich in living memory. The Federal Reserve's QE programme makes money from bond purchases which in five years has more than tripled its balance sheet to more than $3.6 trillion. This makes the Federal Reserve behaviour more akin to a hedge fund than a central bank with the remit of creating financial stability.

Andrew Huszar was the Federal Reserve official who implemented the policy of QE. He resigned when he realised that the real purposes of QE was to drive up the prices of the banks' holdings of debt instruments, to provide the banks with trillions of Dollars at zero cost with which to

16 Ryan, J. (2012), 'The Dollar: Exorbitant or Extortionate Privilege', *Social Europe Journal*, 26 April.

17 Rickards, J. (2011), 'Currency Wars: The Making of the Next Global Crisis', PORTFOLIO.

lend and speculate, and to provide the banks with 'fat commissions from brokering most of the Fed's QE transactions.'[18]

Confidence in the health of the US economy, and therefore the US Dollar, could plunge because of continued large US current-account deficits, an unstable banking sector and an expansionist monetary policy. Chinn and Frankel claim that rankings of international currencies change only very slowly, but when they change they do so with a bang. Although the United States surpassed the United Kingdom in economic size very early (between 1860 and 1875 depending on estimates), the US Dollar did not surpass the Pound as the major international currency until 1945.[19]

The potential geopolitical implications of such a projected shift away from the US Dollar are immense. First, the US will lose its privileged seigniorage position which is the ability to achieve permanently higher returns on foreign assets than the returns paid to foreigners who invest in the US. The current economic crisis has revealed that the US legal framework for the regulation of financial markets and institutions is rather inadequate. Even given the dismal state of the legal framework, the actual performance of key regulators like the Federal Reserve and the Securities and Exchange Commission has been appalling, with astonishing examples of incompetence and regulatory capture.[20]

The US government has taken on massive additional contingent liabilities through its bail out/underwriting of the US financial system. Together with the foreseeable increase in actual Federal government liabilities because of vastly increased future Federal deficits, this implies the need for a future private to public sector resource transfer that is most unlikely to be politically feasible without recourse to inflation. The only alternative is default

18 Huszar, A. (2013), 'Confessions of a Quantitative Easer,' *Wall Street Journal*, November 11.

19 Chinn, M. and Frankel, J. (2007), 'Will the Euro Eventually Surpass the Dollar as Leading International Reserve Currency?' in R. Clarida, *G7 Current Account Imbalances: Sustainability and Adjustment*, NBER Report, Chicago, University of Chicago Press, 283–321.

20 Eichengreen, B. (2009), The Dollar Dilemma: The World's Top Currency Faces Competition. Foreign Affairs, September/October.

on Federal debt. There is little doubt that the Federal authorities will choose the inflation and currency depreciation route over the default route.[21]

There are four reasons why China might worry about a decline in the value of the Dollar that would depreciate the value of their Treasury bill holdings. First, the US government is racking up huge debts in its efforts to climb out of recession and purge the financial system of toxic assets. Massive government debt is a sure-fire means to put downward pressure on a nation's currency value. Second, printing money is a means to relieve temporarily some of the debt problems. However, this always leads to an inflation problem in the long term, which again places a declining bias on the Dollar. Third, US interest rates are at exceptionally low levels. This will reduce the attraction for international investors of holding US Treasury Bills, bonds and notes once the need for 'safety' is deemed to be less pressing. Fourth, there are already signs that the 'safety' effect may be waning. It appears that China is preparing to take a diversification and risk minimising strategy by purchasing other assets such as gold.[22]

The US should consider two practical changes in the current international monetary order. The further evolution of a multi-polar system in which other currencies increasingly share the international position of the Dollar in private markets. The Euro based on a collective European economy as large as the United States' and with capital markets as extensive in most respects, is the most obvious candidate. The Euro already rivals the Dollar in some domains, such as currency holdings and private bond placements, and will become a full competitor whenever the Eurozone countries adopt a more integrated fiscal policy. The Renminbi is likely to acquire a significant international role once China allows it to be converted for financial as well as current account transactions and eases capital controls.

21 Eichengreen, B. (2011), *Exorbitant Privilege: The Rise and Fall of the Dollar*, Oxford and New York, Oxford University Press.

22 Waldmeir, P. (2009), Beijing bets on bullion to diversify foreign reserves. *Financial Times*, 7 May.

Scenario 2: The Euro gains strength slowly in a turbulent world

For a number of commentators in the US and the UK the debt crisis in the Eurozone has reinforced their view that the Euro has always been a bad idea with a finite duration.[23] Outspoken critics of the single currency across the Atlantic such as Martin Feldstein have gone even as far as to encourage Greece to unilaterally leave the single currency and take a temporary 'holiday' from the Eurozone.[24]

Concerns by Brazil, Russia India and China that the US can flood the world with Dollars and finance rising budget deficits at little cost, enhancing the US Dollar's global status and crowding out the borrowing efforts of other countries, echo earlier critiques from Europe. Since the 1960s, France has been a critic of US alleged 'exorbitant privilege' of international reserve asset power.[25] One of the many reasons for the creation of the Euro was indeed to fulfil the Europeans' long-held wish to create a reserve asset that could counter the US Dollar's global dominance. One reason why such a step change could take place is that the US Treasury is indirectly provoking such action through its criticisms of China's alleged manipulation of its currency. In the unlikely event that the People's Bank of China allowed the Renminbi to fall by stopping US Dollar purchases, the Chinese current-account surplus would undoubtedly fall. The reality is that, if monetary hostilities between Beijing and Washington D. C. escalated then the Euro would become part of the collateral damage.

23 The pessimistic views on the euro by US economists in academia and the FED are thoroughly investigated by a European Commission paper by Jonung & Drea (2009) entitled: 'The Euro: It can't happen. It's a bad idea. It won't last: US economists on the EMU, 1989–2002'. A marked exception is Eichengreen (2007; 2009; 2011), who represents the euro-optimist branch among US mainstream economists.

24 Feldstein, M. (2010), 'Let Greece take a eurozone "holiday"', *Financial Times*, February 16. For a European reaction to Feldstein's proposal, see Baldwin, R. and C. Wyplosz (2010) 'How to destroy the Eurozone: Feldstein's euro-holiday idea', VoxEU.

25 Portes, R. (2007), 'The rise of the Euro'. VoxEU.

The introduction of the synthetic Euro in 1999 and then physically in 2002 was the most far-reaching change in the international monetary system since the changeover to floating exchange rates in the early 1970s. Where the Deutschmark and the Yen failed in the 1970s and 1980s, the Euro now appears to have succeeded, namely in challenging the US Dollar as the undisputed leading international currency. The Euro gained considerable clout as an international trade, investment, anchor and reserve currency over recent years. That is why, for the first time in many decades, there is serious debate about whether the US Dollar will remain the premier international currency going forward.[26]

The Euro already has effectively displaced the US Dollar as the key reserve currency of Europe. Eastern European countries, the Nordic countries and Switzerland hold most of their reserves in Euros. The central banks of countries that are members of the Eurozone increasingly hedge their US Dollar holdings.

Scenario 3: Will the Renminbi become a reserve currency

What role will the Renminbi play in the global financial markets in the future? Will it ever become a reserve currency? To be eligible for reserve status, several prerequisites have to be fulfilled:

- The currency should be fully convertible and widely accepted;
- Its financial markets should be broad and liquid;
- Its value should be reasonably stable;
- Large amounts of trade should be transacted in it.[27]

26 Galati, G. and Wooldridge, P. (2006), The Euro as a reserve currency: a challenge to the pre-eminence of the US dollar? BIS Working Paper, No. 218, October.

27 Thimann, C. (2009), 'Global Roles of Currencies'. ECB Working Paper Series, No. 1031.

On 13 March 2009 China's Premier Wen Jiabao expressed concerns about the future of the US Dollar, the currency in which most of his country's official reserves are denominated. His remarks provoked contrasting reactions among US economists. Some, like Fred Bergsten of the Institute of International Economics, exhorted the US government to take Wen's concerns seriously and listen to Beijing's suggestion to create a substitution account in the IMF, which would allow Fund members to exchange unwanted US Dollar balances for Special Drawing Rights (SDRs), as part of a gradual process to replace the US Dollar with a supra-national reserve currency over the long run.[28]

According to other US economists, such as Paul Krugman, China had fallen into a trap of its own making due to its reluctance to adopt a more flexible exchange rate policy in the past. Since any attempt by China or any other country to diversify away from the US Dollar too much or too quickly would be self-defeating, there was no immediate threat to US or world financial stability.[29]

Over the last three decades there have been five co-ordinated interventions in major currencies. In 1985 the G7 signed the Plaza Accord to weaken the US Dollar. In 1987 the G7 changed stance at Louvre and pledged to support the falling US Dollar. Similarly, in 1995 the G7 again decided to intervene to help the US currency. In 1998 the US and Japan sold US Dollars to prop up the Yen. In 2000 the European Central Bank persuaded the Federal Reserve and the Banks of Japan, United Kingdom and Canada to support the Euro.

Four of these five interventions were ultimately successful in changing the trend of the currency markets. In 1985 the US Dollar stopped overshooting against the Yen and the Deutschmark. In 1995 the US Dollar began a sustained rally that lasted throughout the late 1990s. In 1998 the 'Yen carry trade' reversed sharply to the benefit of Japan's currency and in the early 2000s the Euro rarely traded below the levels at which the G7 central banks

28 Bergsten, C. F. (2009), 'We Should Listen to Beijing's Currency Idea'. *Financial Times*, 8 April.

29 Krugman, P. (2009), 'China's Dollar Trap'. *New York Times*, 2 April.

had intervened to support it. The Louvre Accord is the one exception here. Though the G7 agreed in February 1987 to help the US Dollar, it continued to slide as the German Bundesbank raised interest rates in the summer.

China continues to raise questions about the dominance of the US Dollar and the need for an alternative monetary system; other countries have also raised concerns about the viability of the US Dollar. A gradual decline of the US Dollar would be mirrored by a rise in the use of the Renminbi.[30] China has many reasons to try to reduce its exposure to the US Dollar. They include very low yields paid by the US Treasury and a vulnerability to US decisions on managing its debt, which could lead to inflation that would erode the value of those holdings. Even if it is not always publicly acknowledged, China's resolve to reduce its US Dollar exposure has intensified after political fights in the United States over the debt ceiling. They have reinforced worries that the United States could unintentionally slip into a situation where it will default on its obligations.[31]

China's leadership will have to make a hard choice between two different approaches: the US Dollar or the German Euro approach. On the weight and strength of the US economy and military power after the Second World War, the US Dollar was able to topple the Pound Sterling and become a global and dominant currency while pursuing an independent macro-economic policy. If China followed the US Dollar approach, it would lead China to pursue a strategy of having the Renminbi used as an international currency in parallel to the US Dollar, the Euro and, perhaps, the Yen. The second option would be the German Euro approach: currency regionalisation through a series of concrete steps (e.g., a regional currency mechanism like the Exchange Rate Mechanism) in the direction of a single currency replacing a number of individual currencies. If China were to follow this approach, it should involve itself in a fully-fledged monetary

30 Garten, J. (2009), Amid the rubble Shangkong will rise. *Financial Times*, 11 May.

31 Orlik, Tom, Bob Davis (2012), 'Beijing Diversifies Away from US Dollar.' *Wall Street Journal*, 2 March.

union in Asia, and, in the final stage, the Renminbi would be diminished and replaced by a new Asian single currency.[32]

Zhou's declaration of geopolitical intent rather than that of a viable plan to supplant the US Dollar with SDRs, the IMF's unit of account, into a super-sovereign reserve currency never gained momentum even though it remains for some, including John Williamson, an elegant solution to the problem of excessive dependence on the US Dollar. But Beijing's initiative made clear its desire to shape a new monetary order.[33]

The birth of an offshore Renminbi market, principally in Hong Kong, also gives China the chance to monitor the impact of banking and currency reforms in a semi-controlled environment. That is a valuable experience for the day China opens up its domestic financial markets, which many say is Zhou's strategic aim in pushing the internationalisation of the Renminbi.

Starting from scratch in 2009, China was settling 12% of its trade in its own currency by 2013. China is encouraging the use of the Renminbi in overseas investment and is providing ever more official aid and loans in its own currency. The Renminbi is circulating more widely in neighbouring countries, just as the US Dollar is in Latin America and the Euro is in Eastern Europe and North Africa. In Mongolia, the Renminbi accounts for 60% of the local cash in circulation. By October 2013 the PBOC had spun a web of nearly 2.2 trillion Renminbi in credit lines with more than 20 central banks around the world since 2009, including the ECB and the Bank of England. These are designed to keep Renminbi-denominated trade running in case liquidity dries up and to lay the foundations for deeper monetary integration with the signatory countries. In the same vein, at least ten central banks, including those of South Africa, Australia, Nigeria and Malaysia, have invested part of their reserves in Renminbi bonds. Offshore Renminbi markets have sprung up in London, Singapore and Frankfurt. These shifts, which are more symbolic than substantive at present, will

32 Gao Haihong, Yongding Yu (2011), 'The Internationalization of the Renminbi.' Bank for International Settlements Papers, no. 61.

33 Zhou, X. (2009), 'Reform of the International Monetary System', Speeches, People's Bank of China, 23 March.

develop critical mass over time and have the potential to start transforming the global monetary system. The Chinese government's recent policy actions are indicative of its serious intent to broaden the global role if its currency.

Ben Bernanke coined the phrase of 'global savings glut'. The problem is not that China has saved too much, sent its saved money to the US, and this has lowered interest rates there and thus encouraged the American population to over-spend and over-build and over-buy houses.[34] The source of the problem, Zhou explains, is precisely the Triffin dilemma, which is associated with the 'exorbitant privilege' enjoyed by the US. By issuing the main international currency, the US does not have to abide to the laws of macro-economics.[35] There is no disciplinary mechanism that ensures that the twin (current account and budget) deficits of the US are kept under control.[36] This, of course, explains why the US has been able to live well beyond its means for the past 40 years.

China, the largest foreign US creditor, reduced holdings of US Treasury debt in December 2013 by $47.8 billion to $1.27 trillion, the largest decline since December 2011, according to US Treasury Department data released. Until 20 years ago, the Renminbi was so domestic in its use that foreigners in China were supposed to use vouchers called 'foreign-exchange certificates' instead. In April 2014 a long-stalled agreement linking the Hong Kong and Shanghai stock exchanges and allowing trading to be settled in Renminbi got a green light. The market in Renminbi-denominated 'dim sum' bonds issued offshore (mainly in Hong Kong) is growing. Some 18% of China's foreign trade is now settled in Renminbi a proportion the Hong Kong Monetary Authority expects to reach 30% in 2015. Some central banks already hold a small chunk of their countries' foreign-exchange

34 Bernanke, B. (2005), 'The Global Saving Glut and the US Current Account Deficit', Sandridge Lecture, Virginia Association of Economics, Richmond, Virginia, 10 March. Bernanke, B. (2010), 'Rebalancing the Global Recovery', Sixth European Central Bank Central Banking Conference, Frankfurt, 19 November.

35 Zhou, X. (2009), 'Reform of the International Monetary System', Speeches, People's Bank of China, 23 March.

36 Zhang, M. (2009), 'China's New International Financial Strategy amid the Global Financial Crisis', *China & World Economy*, 17 (5), 22–35.

reserves in Renminbi. Economists even talk of an emerging 'Renminbi bloc', encompassing China, Hong Kong, Taiwan and the ten members of the Association of South-East Asian Nations. The globalisation of the Renminbi seems to be picking up momentum.

China as one of the largest exporters undervalues the Renminbi and runs a large trade surplus. What if it decided to take a radical step and go all the way to a 100% reserve gold currency as the ultimate hard currency? The Chinese would need to surpass the Federal Reserve's official, but unaudited, gold holding of 8,133.5 tonnes. This would be a game changer as far as the US Dollar continuing to be the global reserve currency is concerned.

Scenario 4:
Super-sovereign reserve currency – A nice theoretical debate

In late March 2009, US Treasury Secretary Timothy Geithner sent the US Dollar tumbling when he said he was 'actually quite open' to China's proposal for a greater role for SDRs. The US Dollar lost 1.3% against the Euro within 10 minutes of Geithner's unexpected comment.[37]

On 3 March 2009, the Governor of China's Central Bank had called for a 'super-sovereign reserve currency' that would be run by the IMF, an idea that has been backed by Russia, Brazil and India. Losing the global reserve currency status might be healthier for the global economy in the long run, but it would not be a very comfortable adjustment for the US.

The idea of the super sovereign reserve currency would be to create a reserve currency that is disconnected from individual nations and is able to remain stable in the long run, thus removing the inherent deficiencies caused by using credit-based national currencies. This is a clear sign that

37 Bloomberg (2009), 'Geithner Remarks on IMF Currency Roll'. Foreign Exchange Market, 26 March.

China, as the largest holder of US Dollar financial assets, is concerned about the potential inflationary risk of the US Federal Reserve printing money.[38]

China is over-exposed to US Dollar-denominated securities. While the US puts domestic economic needs before its creditors, the Beijing authorities now worry that possible future inflation could cost them dearly. As the Bank of China's Governor says, a reserve super currency could be created through further issuance of the IMF's SDR's – the IMF's in-house reserve asset. The value of SDRs is based on a basket of four currencies – the US Dollar, Yen, Euro and British Sterling – and they are used largely as a unit of account by the IMF and some other international organisations. But the SDR is unlikely to become a reserve currency any time soon. It would take years to develop SDR money markets that are liquid enough to be a reserve asset.

China's proposal would expand the basket of currencies forming the basis of SDR valuation to all major economies and set up a settlement system between SDRs and other currencies so they could be used in international trade and financial transactions. The current international financial system, which is based on a single currency, has two main flaws. First, the reserve-currency status of the US Dollar helped to create global imbalances. Second, the country that issues the reserve currency faces a trade-off between domestic and international stability. Massive money-printing by the Federal Reserve to support the economy makes sense from a national perspective, but it may harm the US Dollar's value.

Some specific steps are needed to improve the role of the SDR as a global reserve asset. In order to make the SDR the principal reserve asset via allocation, close to $3 trillion in SDRs would need to be created. Wijnholds has thus suggested a so-called SDR Substitution Account. The idea is to permit countries whose official US Dollar holdings are larger than they desire to convert US Dollars into SDRs. Conversion would occur outside

38 Eichengreen, B. and Frankel J. (1996), 'The SDR, Reserve Currencies, and the Future of the International Monetary System'. In M. Mussa, J. Boughton, and P. Isard (eds), *The Future of the SDR in Light of Changes in the International Financial System*, Washington D. C., International Monetary Fund.

the market and thus would not put downward pressure on the US Dollar. This suggestion, however, requires settling who will bear the exchange (Dollar) risk as the SDR Substitution Account is likely to mostly hold Dollars as assets.[39]

The SDR is unlikely to be a practical alternative to the US Dollar. In theory, countries can purchase liabilities issued by the IMF that are linked to the SDR. If the objective is to diversify out of US Dollars, reserve managers can achieve it more efficiently by directly increasing their holdings of Euro, Yen and Sterling (the other currencies to which the SDR is linked). More than half of China's reserves are denominated in US Dollars.

Conclusions

The decline in the international role of the US Dollar is caused by persistent current account deficits combined with a long-term decline in the US Dollar's exchange rate – and perhaps imperial overreach, too. The projected speed at which the US Dollar will lose its predominant position as a global reserve currency obviously depends on the US Treasury fiscal policy. Chinese and European leaders frequently emphasise the US responsibilities for the stability of the US Dollar as the premier reserve currency.

It is unclear whether the diversification benefit would be enough to make reserve managers willing to hold SDRs instead of Dollars (or Euros), unless the SDR takes a prominent role as unit of account or medium of exchange in global trade and financial transactions. The use of an SDR in international trade and finance would be painfully slow. Geographical, historic and cultural ties create inertia in the currencies chosen as units of account in international trade and finance.

Are the US Dollar's days as reserve currency over? No. But they are numbered. In the past a strong and open US financial system helped

39 Wijnholds, O. (2009), 'The Dollar's Last Days?' Project Syndicate.org.

facilitate the US Dollar's international use. While a connection naturally exists between the US Dollars' role in trade and the growth of an accommodating financial structure, US financial markets had the reputation of being innovative and relatively free of tighter regulation. Their breadth and depth enhance the liquidity of US Dollar-denominated assets. Moreover, as US trade expand and US financial markets grow, more and more foreign financial firms – even ones not located in the US – offer US Dollar-denominated products. All this makes holding US Dollars convenient and transacting in US Dollars relatively easy.

China has now decided to start looking for a smooth exit from the game. The Central Bank of China announced that it is no longer in China's favour to accumulate foreign-exchange reserves. The internationalisation of the Renminbi will include its use in settling trade and financial deals. The Renminbi is well advanced as is the liberalisation of China's capital account so that the Renminbi can be freely converted with other currencies at market rates. Without that convertibility, much deeper domestic financial markets and a floating exchange-rate, the Renminbi will not achieve becoming a global reserve currency, such as the Dollar, Euro, Yen, Sterling or Swiss franc.

Arguably, what ultimately defines the US Dollar's dominant status is the US government's fiscal capacity to back the Federal Reserve's provision of US Dollar liquidity at times of crisis. This capacity is certain to decline as the global economy expands and demand for US Dollar assets increases; the United States will inevitably see its reserve-currency monopoly eroded. It could therefore only be a matter of time before the global monetary system becomes multi-polar.

Timescales matter. According to the European Central Bank, the global economy is already close to operating with three regional exchange rate anchors – the US Dollar, the Euro and the Renminbi – so the transition to a multi-polar system could occur sooner than is sometimes asserted. Nevertheless, given the importance of financial deepening and integration in the internationalisation of currencies, any shift will still be gradual.

MIGUEL OTERO-IGLESIAS

4 The Battle for the Euro! China's (Information) Strategy to Steer Market Sentiment in Favour of the Single Currency

Introduction

In the age of information, media outlets have considerable influence in shaping public perceptions. This is especially true in highly interconnected financial markets where instant information can suddenly change investment decisions. Throughout the Eurozone sovereign debt crisis, European policymakers have blamed the Anglo-American press for scaremongering over the faith of the Euro. The possibility of a Euro break-up has been constant news in the openly Euro-sceptic British tabloids but also in the editorially more balanced *Financial Times*, *The Economist*, *The New York Times* and the *Wall Street Journal*. By contrast, the Chinese Government and its associated agency *Xinhua* have had a very different approach. Every time the Euro has fallen into a danger zone, the Chinese leadership has counterbalanced widespread Euro-scepticism by propping up the single currency. It has been widely publicised that China has supported the Eurozone with tangible investments in debt bonds of troubled Eurozone countries. However, what has been overlooked by the literature in International Relations and International Political Economy is how China has also developed a carefully designed communication strategy to steer market sentiment in favour of the Euro. While covering China's financial support to the Eurozone, this chapter will also focus on this less studied informational support. By matching Chinese public (media and official) statements of support with the foreign exchange rate trajectory of the Euro, it will be demonstrated that China has had great influence in sustaining the value of the European currency.

The chapter is structured in two main parts. The first, which is more descriptive, presents a detailed recompilation of China's informational and actual support to the Euro since its birth until present days. It will show how Chinese policymakers stepped in to sustain the value of the European currency every time it was under considerable market pressure during the 2010–12 Eurozone sovereign debt crisis. The strategy has been two-fold. On the one hand, the Chinese leadership has used public statements or commentaries in the state-owned Xinhua news agency to show their confidence in the single currency, and on the other, they have accelerated their diversification moves out of the Dollar and into the Euro. China's behaviour has changed market perceptions on the Euro, as recognised by financial heavy weights such as George Soros, who does not shy away from claiming that effectively China saved the Euro. The second part of the chapter is more analytical. The main aim is to explain why China is supporting the Euro and the European integration project at large. Several reasons are explored. China needs to diversify out of the Dollar, so this is good opportunity to accelerate this process. China has already over $800bn in Euro-denominated assets hence it needs to protect the value of its assets. The EU is China's most important market. Therefore it is in China's own national interest to stabilise the European market. Finally, this crisis is a good opportunity for China to present itself in front of its European counterparts as a reliable and trustworthy partner and consequently it should be granted market economy status and more saying in global economic and financial affairs.

The Record of China's Informational and Financial Support to the Euro

The main objective in this first part is to document China's approach toward the European currency since its creation. It is a descriptive section. The analysis of why this is the case will come in the second part of the paper. The main goal here is to present in a chronological fashion how Chinese policymakers' strong support to the Euro has been consistent over the years.

China welcomes the arrival of the Euro

From the early days of European Monetary Union (EMU), the emergence of the Euro as a potential challenger to the Dollar was greeted favourably by the Chinese government. In 1999, year of the launch of the single currency, the Foreign Minister of China, Tang Jiaxuan, stated: 'We believe that the birth of the Euro will help advance the process of European integration and establish a more balanced international financial and monetary system' (Tang 1999). Chinese policymakers have never been completely satisfied with Dollar unipolarity in monetary affairs and thus they welcomed the Euro as a counter-balancing project with the potential to help them diversify their national savings in different currencies. For them, the Euro would bring more choice and therefore more stability to the system. This belief was widely shared in East Asia, as Xu Mingqi notes:

> Generally speaking, East Asians were not as sceptical as Americans when the EU embarked on [...] the Euro. East Asians welcomed the Euro basically for two reasons: the first was that it would be more convenient and efficient for them to do business and travel around the EU countries with a single, unified currency; and the second was the hope that the Euro, backed by the EU's economic size and strength would eventually become an alternative choice of international currency vis-à-vis the US Dollar (Xu 2007:273).

This interpretation has been reinforced in subsequent years. In 2002, when the Euro was physically launched, Xiang Huaicheng, the Chinese Minister of Finance, called for more diversification into the Euro by saying: 'It's better to put all our eggs in varied baskets rather than a single one. I might suggest to my colleagues in other government departments to buy more Euros. Obviously the Euro is getting stronger these days ... no one will doubt the success of the Euro' (MoCoC 2002). In 2005, the Chinese Prime Minister, Wen Jiabao, continued saying that a successful Euro would bring a more stable system, and thus China would 'support the role of the

Euro in maintaining international financial stability' (Wen 2005). During the same period the governor of the People's Bank of China (PBoC), Zhou Xiaochuan, declared: 'We have long attached importance to the holding of a certain amount of Euro assets' (*Xinhua* 2005), indicating that Chinese foreign exchange reserves should be invested in different currencies other than the Dollar to avoid exchange rate risks.

With $3.2 trillion of foreign reserves accumulated over the past decade, diversification of currencies has always been one of the main aims of the Chinese government. In this regard the European currency has become the main alternative to the US Dollar. This has been acknowledged in 2007, still before the global financial crisis, by the deputy governor of the PBoC, Wu Xiaoliang, by saying that 'with the economic development of the European Union and the stability of the Euro, the increasing proportion of Euros in reserves of central banks is an inevitable trend' (*Xinhua* 2007).

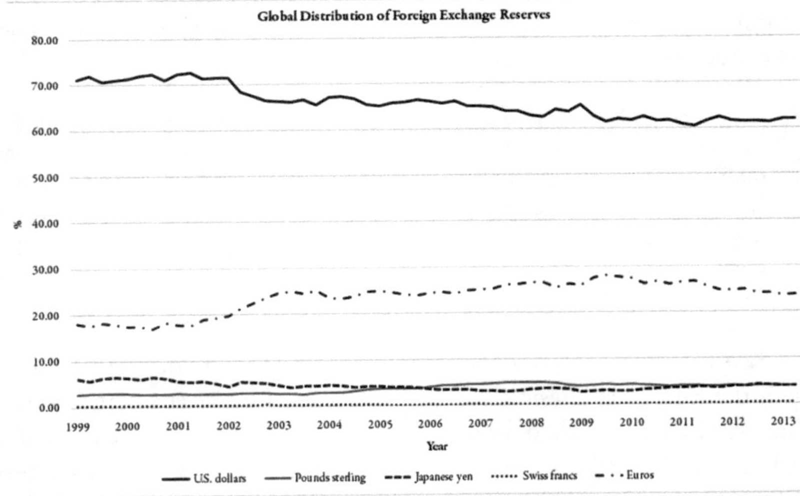

Figure 1: Global distribution of global foreign exchange reserves. Source: COFER, IMF.

China's currency distribution of foreign reserves is a state secret, nonetheless in an article published in 2010 in the *China Securities Journal*, an official publication, unnamed managers from the State Administration of

Foreign Exchange (SAFE), the state agency in charge of managing the foreign exchange reserves, disclosed that China's reserves were roughly similar to the global average (see Figure 1). 65% are in US Dollars, 26% in Euros, 5% in British pounds and 3% in Japanese Yen (*Reuters* 2010).

China does not believe in the 'Euro-break-up' theory

While lingering in the background since the creation of the Euro, the likelihood of a possible break-up of the Eurozone has resurfaced with force during the current financial crisis, especially since it became obvious in early 2010 that Greece was unable to meet its debt obligations. During that time reports and Op-Eds hinting at the possibility of a break-up of EMU were commonplace in the international financial media coming out of New York and London (Allen 2010; Harui 2010; Heaney 2010; Klaus 2010; Krugman 2010; Rachman 2010). Policymakers in Europe denounced that there was an Anglo-Saxon media campaign to undermine the single currency. While this might sound a bit too conspiratorial, the truth is that for longstanding Euro-sceptics, coincidently a large number of them based in the US and the UK, the fiscal troubles of the Eurozone periphery – which are still acute as of the time of writing – only prove that they were right about the structural shortcomings of the Eurozone project. For many of them the Achilles heel of EMU is that, in addition to not being an Optimum Currency Area (OCA), it is a currency union without the necessary federal fiscal budget to transfer funds from less hit to more financially troubled regions. For a number of commentators in the US and the UK the debt crisis in the Eurozone has reinforced their view that the Euro has always been a bad idea with a finite duration.[1] Outspoken critics of the single currency across the Atlantic such as Martin Feldstein have gone even as far

1 The pessimistic views on the Euro by US economists in academia and the FED are thoroughly investigated by a European Commission paper by Jonung & Drea (2009) entitled: 'The Euro: It can't happen. It's a bad idea. It won't last: US economists on the EMU, 1989–2002'. A marked exception is Eichengreen (2007; 2009; 2011), who represents the Euro-optimist branch among US mainstream economists.

as to encourage Greece to unilaterally leave the single currency and take a temporary 'holiday' from the Eurozone (Feldstein 2010).[2]

This rather pessimistic outlook on the Euro contrasts with the beliefs put forward by Chinese policymakers and commentators. For an overwhelming majority of Chinese financial elites and scholars interviewed in China in 2009 the likelihood of an Eurozone break-up is extremely remote. They acknowledge that by not having a full-fledged fiscal union there will always be doubts about the project, but a dismembering of the Eurozone is very unlikely in their opinion.[3] Some would even criticise Anglo-Saxon media, commentators and scholars for giving too much credit to this possibility. Zhou Hong, director of the Institute of European Studies at the Chinese Academy of Social Sciences, for example, denounces the scaremongering of American commentators as a US strategy to split the Europeans in order to weaken them (Zhou H. 2009). She was not the only one with this opinion.

Most policymakers and financial elites in China think that leaving the Euro would be too costly economically and politically for any country in the Eurozone. Besides, they are convinced that the Europeans will deepen their integration process because this is the only way that they can maintain their influence in the world. For a lot of these elites it comes down to a survival instinct. The Europeans will realise that they can only survive if they integrate further, if they split up, they will perish. The influential Yu Yongding, former member of the monetary committee of the PBoC, summarises well the general impression of the Chinese financial elites on the future of the single currency. In his view there are two possible options: the Eurozone integrates further and creates common economic governance or it goes backwards and the union disintegrates. He predicts the latter as the most likely scenario. 'History shows us that monetary unions are very fragile in times of crises. This is true. But history is only good to explain

2 For a European reaction to Feldstein's proposal, see Baldwin and Wyplosz (2010), 'How to destroy the Eurozone: Feldstein's Euro-holiday idea'.

3 While it can be argued that these interviews were taken before the crisis in the Eurozone periphery reached its peak, I have tried to follow the debates in China very closely since then and the general view remains bullish on the survival of the Euro. See below.

history, not to explain the future. I think the Euro is here to stay' (Yu 2009). This optimistic take on the Euro coincides with the research results on Chinese perceptions on the EU by Zhu Liqun, a Chinese IR scholar. She also finds that the 'Chinese are optimists and like to believe that "the road is tortuous, but the future is bright"' when it comes to describing European integration, which they see as 'irreversible' (Zhu 2008:150–1).

China's public relations support to the Euro

Chinese policymakers' optimism on the future of the Euro is also reflected in their actions. That the Euro was able to maintain its exchange rate value above the US Dollar even in the midst of its greatest existential crisis is partly due to Chinese confidence in the long term consolidation of the single currency. One of the most critical moments in the 12 years of Euro history came on 26 May 2010 in the midst of the Greek debt crisis when a report by the *Financial Times* disclosed that China's SAFE was 'reviewing its holdings of Eurozone debt in the wake of the crisis' (Oakley & Anderlini 2010). At that moment, the up to €750bn strong European Financial Stability Facility (EFSF) had finally been agreed but the Euro was continuing in free fall approaching the $1.20 mark from over $1.50 at the end of 2009 (see Figure 2).

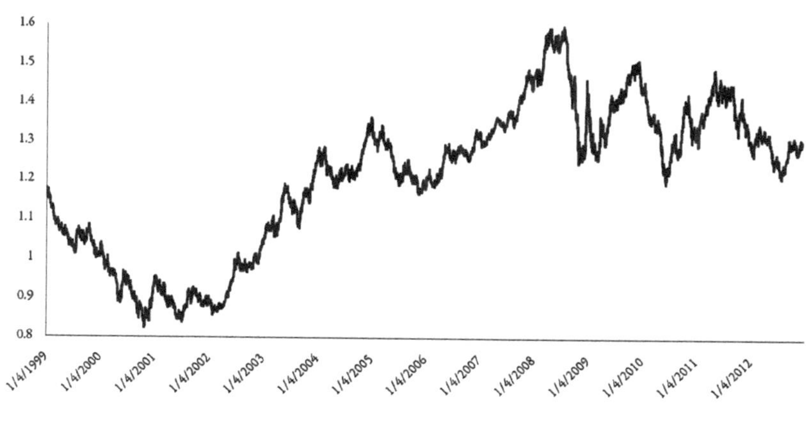

Figure 2: Euro-Dollar Exchange rate (1999–2012 March). Source: ECB.

Once the *FT* report was published, the reaction of the markets was imminent and the single currency plunged another 1.5%, nearing a four-year low against the greenback. Confidence in the Euro was vanishing. However, in what can only be interpreted as a coordinated public relations rescue action, the Chinese government stepped in and stabilised the value of the Euro in a decisive moment. Only hours after the *FT* report was published, in an unusual statement for its uniqueness in responding to media rumours (Li et al. 2010), SAFE labelled the report as 'groundless' and stressed that as a 'responsible long-term investor and, under the principle of maintaining diversified investments, Europe has been and will continue to be one of the major markets for investing China's exchange reserves' (Anderlini & Oakley 2010). To eliminate any shadow of doubt, the same day the president of China Investment Corporation (CIC), the Chinese sovereign wealth fund, also came out publicly in defence of the single currency by saying that 'CIC will keep its investment level in Europe, no more, no less. Short-term fluctuations won't bring serious effect on us' (cited in Anderlini & Oakley 2010). Chinese official Euro-support did not stop there. Just a few days later, the president of another big Chinese investment fund, the National Social Security Fund, Dai Xianglong, also backed the single currency against speculative attacks by saying that the Eurozone's sovereign debt crisis was only temporary and that the more long term worry was 'future turbulence in the Dollar as a result of widening deficits in the US' (cited in Dennis 2010). The Chinese strategy to help the Euro did finally work. The single currency reached a bottom of $1.1942 on 8 June 2010 and it bounced back to over $1.30 less than a month later.

China saves the Euro in its moment of need

The influence of China in holding up the European currency was acknowledged by none other than the renowned investor George Soros who declared shortly after these events that 'China saved the Euro'. In his words, 'once it was discovered that China was a buyer, the Euro jumped from its value of $1.20 to $1.30'. After this move, Soros' perceptions on the future of the Euro changed. Before, the possibility of a break-up of the Euro was in his mind (Allen 2010), but after 'China had a role to play in its survival', his opinion changed to a more optimist outlook on the integrity of the Eurozone (White 2010). This is a significant in change in perceptions since Soros was reported to have been in the dinner of hedge fund managers who decided in February 2010 to bet against the Euro (Pulliam et al. 2010). It seems that Soros, and presumably many other investors bearish on the single currency, changed his faith on the Euro after being 'burned' by China's informational and actual financial Euro-support strategy. His comments certainly hint in that direction.

Since summer 2010 China has openly shown its support to the single currency, verbally and by declaring openly that it is buying and will continue to buy bonds from the countries in the Eurozone periphery. In July 2010 it was leaked that it made a $1bn offer to buy Spanish debt (Oakley & Sakoui 2010), in August 2010 Yu Yongding, speaking informally on behalf of the PBoC, declared that his nation had bought 'quite a lot' of European bonds (Zachariahs & Harui 2010), and in October 2010 China was reported to have invested first in Greek (*Handelsblatt* 2010) and then in Portuguese debt (Wise 2010). In November 2010, at the time when Ireland had to be bailed out (another critical moment in the Euro crisis) the Chinese state-owned news agency *Xinhua* published an editorial entitled: 'Euro will not fail', counteracting again Anglo-Saxon scaremongering on the bleak future for the European currency. Yet again the Chinese authorities were keen to change market perception on the Euro by stating:

> Contrary to the widespread claim that the Eurozone is doomed to break up, the single currency will not fail, although it is facing the toughest challenge since its birth in 1999 ... As a major achievement of European integration, the Euro is a landmark in the world's monetary history. It has become the second largest reserve currency as well as the second most traded currency in the world after the U. S. Dollar. Despite its shortcomings, which have been exposed by the debt crisis, the Euro has brought economic benefits and currency stability to its members. A breakup of the Eurozone would be politically unacceptable (*Xinhua* 2010).

Again we see here a clear correlation between the Euro-Dollar exchange rate and Chinese determined public support for the European currency. Between 4 November and 29 November 2010, the day the *Xinhua* editorial was published, the Euro plunged from $1.424 to $1.314. Coincidently after 30 November 2010 the European currency entered a new rally reaching again a new high of $1.48 in April 2011 (see Figure 2).

The Chinese support to the Euro continued in 2011. In January of that year the visit of the likely-to-be next Premier of China Li Keqiang to Spain was surrounded by rumours that China would invest €6bn in Spanish debt (Mallet & Wiesmann 2011). In April, when the Spanish Prime Minister José Luis Rodriguez Zapatero visited China, the current Chinese Premier Wen Jiabao restated China's willingness to buy further Spanish debt, making Spanish analysts believe that China holds now approximately 12% of overall Spanish government debt (Junquera 2011). The success of China's strategy of making the investment community believe that it stands behind the Euro was confirmed in February 2011 when the *Financial Times* chief correspondent on international finance Henny Sender (2011) wrote a piece suggesting that the reason behind the exchange rate strength of the Euro vis-à-vis the greenback was that 'the Chinese have been buying European sovereign debt in a big and – for China – very public way'.

China supports the Euro by word and deed

Up to that point, it was difficult to say whether China's support to the Euro was mainly a public relations campaign or a genuine investment strategy. However, a few months later, in June 2011 Standard Chartered Bank confirmed earlier estimations that China was actively diversifying out of the Dollar and buying more Euro-denominated debt (Anderlini & Dalloway 2011). Since then and up to the time of writing (March 2012) the two trends have continued. Chinese officials have publicly shown their support to the European currency and an increased number of studies point to the fact that China has indeed increased its purchases of Euro-denominated debt. In October 2011, again in a phase when the Euro was under considerable market pressure with risks spreads rising between Italian and Spanish 10 year debt bonds and German Bunds, Chinese officials renewed their public confidence in Europe. Ahead of the annual EU-China meeting (which the EU authorities postponed until February 2012 due to the gravity of the crisis in Europe), Jiang Yu, a spokeswoman of the Ministry of Foreign Affairs of China, declared that 'we have said many times that we support the measures Europe has taken to deal with the financial crisis ... We believe these difficulties are temporary, and that European countries can reach unanimity and have sufficient ability and financial strength to resolve their own issues' (cited in Blanchard 2011). A few weeks later, the Minister of Foreign Affairs of China Yang Jiechi repeated the same message: 'We believe that Europe has the complete wisdom and ability to solve the debt problem ... China has always supported Europe's response to the international financial crisis and its economic recovery efforts' (cited in Wee 2011).

In March 2012, Tom Orlik and Bob Davies (2012) from the *Wall Street Journal* calculated that China had effectively diversified substantially its newly acquired foreign reserves between June 2010 and June 2011. While previously 65% of new purchases would be Dollar denominated instruments in line with the overall distribution of the accumulated stock, during the period of study, Dollar denominated assets would only count for 54% of total purchases. The authors explain this drop by pointing to China's increased interests in Euro-denominated assets. They highlight that at the postponed EU-China summit in February 2012 Premier Wen Jiabao declared that 'Europe is a main investment destination for China to diversify its foreign-exchange rates'. They also point out that from October 2011 onward Klaus Regling, the CEO of the European Financial Stability Facility (EFSF), has been in close talks with officials from SAFE to increase China's participation in the fund. While it is unknown how much China has actually invested in the EFSF, 'documents show that Asia, apart from Japan – essentially China – accounted for between 14% and 24% of purchases for three EFSF bond sales worth €13 billion in the first half of 2011', and as the authors remind us, 'that was before Mr. Regling's Beijing trip', which means that China might have increased its share since then.

Finally, in March 2012 the vice-governor of the PBoC and head of SAFE, Yi Gang confirmed that China has propped up the European currency in the past two years by buying more Euro-denominated debt (cited in Wang & Liu 2012). He summarised China's position on this matter with the following words: 'We believe that Europe will ultimately overcome the debt crisis through their own efforts as well as with the help from the international community. China will continue to be a "long-term and responsible" investor in Europe'. For Yi, concerns over safety, liquidity and potential revenues are three major factors affecting the Chinese government's thinking when it tries to diversify its $3.2 trillion foreign reserve portfolio, and 'under such principles, we will continue our investment in Europe'. In this same intervention Yi confirmed that China has invested in peripheral European debt and that it has been a profitable investment, not least because inflation has remained low in the Eurozone. 'The revenue was higher than the local inflation rate despite the uncertainties of the debt crisis and economic recovery across the region, which proves diversification worked well'. In principle, this means that China will continue to buy European debt.

Explaining China's support to the Euro

After the previous more descriptive account of China's support to the Euro over the past years through both a public relations campaign and actual purchases of debt from the Eurozone peripheral countries with financial difficulties, in this section the aim will be to explain this support. Why is China so confident in the long term success of the European currency and why is it willing to invest such large sums in the project?

China's confidence in European integration

Ultimately Chinese confidence in the Euro is derived from what China scholar Shambaugh (2008:128) calls 'cognitive dissonance', which is 'the natural proclivity to selectively look for confirmation of one's pre-existing beliefs and to reject evidence that contradicts these beliefs'. Chinese financial elites dismiss the idea of a Euro break-up because they believe in the construction of a multi-polar world order out of US hegemony. In this ideal scenario they want to see a strong, united and independent EU pole with enough strength to act as a counterbalance to the US. The Euro is the vivid representation of this, and therefore the possibility of its demise is rejected. The debt crisis in Europe has shown Chinese policymakers that perhaps they were too Euro-optimistic. European economic and political integration is still far behind what they thought. In some aspects Chinese views on Europe have been to a certain degree naïve, but this does not change the fact that overall China is quite positive on the future of Europe, not least because Europe and China have many similarities. Both are ancient civilisations that extend over an entire continent. They can both claim that they are or want to be united in diversity. China like the EU is conformed by different ethnicities, with different cultures and languages. In some ways both are semi-federal structures which face similar challenges and tensions because of their internal differences and disparities (Song 2010). Arguably, if the EU would split up, regionalist forces would gain further momentum in China. This is a scenario that Chinese authorities would like to avoid. By supporting the European integration project they are doing precisely that.

Diversification of foreign reserves

Another reason which explains why China has been supporting the Euro is the fact that China has become over-dependent on the Dollar. The value of the greenback has been in structural decline for some time and this is a major worry in Beijing since roughly ⅔ of the $3.2 trillion of foreign reserves are allocated in Dollar denominated assets. Diversification has become a major imperative and the Euro is the only alternative to the US Dollar. An FX market player with the fire capacity of China has limited choices when it comes to diversifying its assets. It needs a deep, broad and liquid market to allocate its FX investments. China cannot diversify large amounts of its foreign exchange reserves in Canadian, Australian or New Zeeland Dollar because it would collapse these currencies in a matter of days if not hours. The same can be said of gold which has reached record levels in recent times. Even international reserve currencies such as the Swiss franc, the Japanese Yen and the British pound would have limited absorption capacity. The only other currency that can cope with Chinese diversification is the Euro, and even so it has its ceilings. When the European currency reached $1.60 to the Dollar in mid-2008 (see Figure 2) the competitiveness of Eurozone exporters, especially of those based in the Eurozone periphery who are more sensitive to FX variations, suffered severely. In some way it is possible to argue that the desire to diversify out of the Dollar and the consequent demand for Euro-denominated assets was one of the causes of the Eurozone debt crises (Vermeiren 2011). The appreciation-bias of the Euro has eroded the competitiveness of the Eurozone periphery and consequently enlarged the currency account deficits of countries such as Greece, Portugal, Spain and Italy.

The over-dependency of China and the international monetary system at large on the Dollar was clearly visible during the credit crunch crisis of 2008. In the two quarters that followed the collapse of the investment bank Lehman Brothers in September 2008 Dollar liquidity dried up due to the deleveraging operations of major US financial institutions and the risk aversion behaviour of international investors. The necessary blood in the operations of world trade was missing and this meant a collapse in import orders of Chinese products and the consequent dismissal of 20 million Chinese workers. As the governor of the PBoC Zhou Xiaochuan (2009) has pointed out, the global financial crisis has shown again that the international monetary system dominated by the Dollar has an inherent flaw, called the Triffin dilemma. By being the issuer of the world's currency, the US needs to run current account deficits. This in turn means that global imbalances are continuously generated in the system. First these imbalances were with Western Europe, then with Japan and now with China. To avoid this, the international community should promote the use of the IMFs Special Drawing Rights (SDRs), which is a basket composed of the Dollar, the Euro, the Yen and pound sterling. However, Beijing knows that this is a long-term and difficult process, not least because the US is unwilling to support the idea. Therefore, the only other option is to promote other international currencies and until the Chinese RMB matches its full potential, the Euro is the only alternative in town.

Preserving the value of Euro-denominated debt

Apart from diversifying more of its Dollar denominated assets into Euros, China also needs to worry about the value of the Euros that it already has. As mentioned, in 2010 sources within SAFE disclosed that approximately 26% of China's foreign exchange reserves were allocated in Euro-denominated instruments. If we believe that China has continued to gradually diversify out of the Dollar since then, this percentage might be even larger today. But even assuming that this is the actual figure, considering that China has $3.2 trillion in reserves, this means that its Euro holdings are over $800bn. To put this into context, the proposed permanent European Stability Mechanism (ESM), the de facto European Monetary Fund that will substitute in June 2012 the current European Financial Stability Facility, will only have €500. At the current Euro-Dollar exchange rate of $1.32 the fund would have $660, which is still lower than China's holdings in Euros. In other words, and to borrow a phrase widely used in recent times, the Euro has become 'too big to fail' for China. By being the second most used international currency, the European currency is in a similar position as the greenback. Essentially, it has become systemically important. Thus, the same arguments that are used in the US to explain why China will not pull the plug on the Dollar (Krugman 2009) can be applied to the Euro. China needs to keep the value of the Euro up to avoid losses in its existing Euro-denominated holdings.

The importance of the European market

China's calculations are not only focused on maintaining the value of the Euro to keep the purchasing power of its national wealth allocated in Euro-denominated products. It also needs a strong Euro to maintain its export competitiveness in the Eurozone and the EU at large. The EU is actually China's main export market so if the Euro depreciates vis-à-vis the RMB,

Chinese products will be in less demand. This is an important factor because China is still largely dependent on its exporting sector to keep unemployment low. Furthermore, the EU market is important for Chinese exports but also for its imports. The EU is the main provider of high value added technology to China. Therefore China has an intrinsic interest in maintaining economic, political and social stability in the Eurozone.

Providing financial aid to a continent with a per capita income much higher than China's is not a popular option among the Chinese public. Many commentators in China have ridiculed the suggestion that a poor China should help a rich Europe (Xie 2011). But despite this criticism, the Chinese authorities have felt obliged to support the consumption and productive capacity of the European market. As Premier Wen Jiabao explained in February 2012, when German Chancellor Angela Merkel visited Beijing, help to Europe is not only in the interests of the Europeans but also beneficial for China. As he explains: 'Now Europe is facing a debt crisis and we must consider relations with Europe strategically to protect our national interests. On the one hand, our biggest export market is Europe. On the other hand, Europe is our biggest source for importing technology. From this perspective, helping to stabilise European markets in fact amounts to helping ourselves. We must make all quarters of society understand this point' (cited in Buckley 2012).

The Euro crisis provides a good opportunity for China to invest further in the European continent. Chinese businesses are eager to acquire European companies in order to improve their knowledge and capacity in high technology, professional management and international branding. While before the 2010 Euro debt crisis China's foreign direct investment in Europe would not reach €2bn, this figure has been increasing exponentially since then (Godement et al. 2011).

Increasing the political influence in Europe

The reasons behind China's support to the Euro are certainly not only of economic nature. Politics plays an important role too. By supporting the Euro and the Eurozone in a moment of crisis, the Chinese government is seeking to augment its political influence in Europe and gain the Europeans as allies in economic and monetary governance disputes. This was proven in the 2010 meeting between Wen Jiabao and the Euro-troika officials, shortly after it became evident that China had stepped in to stabilise the Euro. Unlike on other occasions when the main theme was the appreciation of the RMB, as demanded for some time by the US, this time ECB president Trichet and his colleagues had to perform a balancing act between their demands and their explicit gratitude for China's 'confidence in sovereign treasuries in Europe' (Grajewski & Taylor 2010). Since that meeting, Europe, unlike the US, has restrained from publicly criticising the underappreciation of the Chinese RMB.

By September 2011, after more than a year of verbal and actual support to the European currency, China started to ask openly for some returns for its help. Granting China market economy status became one of the key demands. Again the thinking of Chinese policymakers was channelled via the state agency *Xinhua* which in a commentary stated that

> Since the eruption of the global financial crisis and the debt crisis in Europe, China has offered help to Europe ... Since last year, China has purchased bonds of several European countries, trying to save nations deep in a debt crisis ... By contrast, it is a pity that the EU side still shows no sincerity on the issue of recognising China's market economy status ... The earlier that the EU announces its recognition, the earlier it could demonstrate its sincerity towards China, winning more popularity and friendship among Chinese people (Wu 2011).

This commentary makes reference to the 5th Summer Davos Forum held in September 2011, just a few weeks before the G20 Summit in Cannes, when Chinese Premier Wen Jiabao publicly, and in a high profile event, put pressure on Europe by saying that China would like to provide aid by increasing its investment in Europe. However, this help would not come for free. He urged European leaders to admit China's status as a market economy. These demands by Chinese policymakers have been interpreted by some as a strategy of taking advantage of Europe in its moment of need. It is argued that China's Euro debt buying campaign has been a well-orchestrated public relations strategy aimed at increasing China's political influence in Europe with little cost. Godement et al. (2011) argue for example that, unlike in the US, in Europe there is no transparency regarding who holds European sovereign debt so China can claim that it has been buying European debt without any public disclosure of these purchases. On the other side, European member states might use this lack of transparency for their own benefits. They might claim that China has invested in their bonds while this is actually not true. While more transparency in European debt markets would certainly be welcomed, it is doubtful whether China's strategy was exclusively a PR campaign. As was presented above, there are a number of studies that argue in favour of China's diversification into the European currency. This would certainly explain why the Euro has maintained its exchange rate value throughout the crisis.

If China has indeed increased its purchases of European debt and at the same time 'saved the Euro', as George Soros claims, it is understandable that China asks for some favours from Europe, and it is also perfectly probable seeing Europe conceding some ground in certain areas. In the last EU-China Summit, for instance, the two parts have agreed to review China's market economy status. This appears to be a concession of the Europeans to the Chinese. The market economy status issue might not be the only that the Chinese authorities might to negotiate in exchange for financial help. It is very likely that Beijing might use this opportunity to ask Europe to lift the arms embargo or to reduce its voting power in the IMF so that emerging markets, including China, have a greater say. Sino-European collaboration has already been at work behind the competition for the new IMF director after Dominique Strauss Kahn's resignation. It seems that China was one of the biggest supporters of Lagarde to head the IMF despite widespread demands for a non-European candidate. One possible reason is that the Chinese and French governments reached an agreement by which Beijing would support Lagarde and in exchange Lagarde would make Min Zhu, a Chinese official and economist, her deputy.

The desire for a G-3 world

While certain influential US commentators in International Relations such as Zbigniew Brzezinski have proposed a G-2 formed by the US and

China as the main decision-making body in international affairs, this is a proposal that does not find great support among Chinese policymakers (Jian 2009). As mentioned above, China prefers to develop a multipolar world and Europe is seen as an important pole in the new configuration. As Khanna and Leonard (2011) indicate, China prefers to have a G-3 world and this is another reason why it has supported the Euro and the Eurozone during the current crisis. Chinese officials recognise that great part of the multilateral order that has emerged in the past fifty years is due to European efforts. When it comes to promoting coordination and cooperation, the enforcement of the rule of law and the pooling of sovereignty at the supranational level Europe has certainly decades of expertise. China respects this legacy.

A triangular relationship in the management of world affairs would also be of China's liking because a triangular power balance is synonym of stability in traditional Chinese culture. This is reflected in how Chinese policymakers think about the future of the international monetary system for instance. The words of Qin Yaqing, senior advisor to the Ministry of Foreign Affairs of China, are a good summary of the general feeling in China. Asked about the future prospects of the European currency, he answers as follows:

> I think the Euro will become a leading currency with the Dollar and I also think that this is a positive development. Only one currency can bring stability but also instability. I am of the belief that a few currencies can bring more stability to the system. This is what I would call the benefits of 'benign competition'. In my belief in the future we will have three major currencies: the Dollar, the Euro and a currency in Asia (either the RMB or a common currency). In East Asia there is now a strong commitment to use local currencies in order to avoid further exposure against the Dollar, this shows that a multi-polar currency system is in demand (Qin 2009).

By supporting the Euro, Chinese officials are moving one step forward towards this triangular configuration. The other big step is to internationalise the RMB, but here too quite significant process has been achieved. As Barry Eichengreen (2011) argues, it is quite likely that in 10 to 15 years, the international monetary system will be a tripolar monetary system. Whether this configuration will be more stable than current Dollar unipolarity is beyond the scope of this article.

By stretching its helping hand to Europe, China is also starting to show that it wants to be a responsible and trustworthy partner in international affairs. China's strategy has been quite measured in many regards. Instead of presenting itself as Europe's 'white knight', it has insisted in the argument that China can certainly help, but ultimately it is down to the Europeans to solve their own crisis. China is in a similar position as Germany. It knows that it has the financial capacity to rescue the Eurozone periphery, but it is also aware that the long-term solution for Europe lies in the improvement of the competitiveness of weaker countries through structural reforms and in the strengthening of the governance structures of the Eurozone in order to establish some sort of fiscal union. This overall strategy was again leaked through an editorial in the state-controlled *Xinhua* agency published shortly after the EFSF head Klaus Regling visited Beijing in October 2011. In this commentary, which is quite likely to reflect the views of the Chinese leadership, one can read that China's purchase of European debt is a positive signal, especially because

> Beijing's good-will gesture is a good response to those who see China as a threatening rival to Europe. Despite differences in politics, economy and culture, China and the EU are still good friends and partners ... However, amid such an unprecedented crisis in Europe, China can neither take up the role as a saviour to the Europeans, nor provide a "cure" for the European malaise ... Obviously, it is up to the European countries themselves to tackle their financial problems. But China can do within its capacity to help as a friend (*Xinhua* 2011).

In many ways Chinese policymakers are quite frustrated about the slowness of the Europeans in tackling the Euro crisis. In their view Europe should be much faster in its political integration project in order to overcome the crisis. Ultimately, in their view, the Euro can only survive if there is a political union behind it to underpin it. This eagerness for accelerating the process of reform is certainly striking. No-one else more than Chinese policymakers should understand that it takes considerable amounts of time to establish a political union out of different nation states with different cultures and traditions. The long history of China is a case in point.

Conclusion

The aim of this chapter has been twofold. First, to present an exhaustive summary of China's support to the Euro since its birth up to the current Euro sovereign debt crisis. Afterwards, to explain why China is interested in a strong Euro. Differently to widespread perceptions in the Anglo-American world that the Euro is doomed, policymakers and financial elites in China believe in the long-term sustainability of the European single currency and this sentiment is reflected in their actions. As George Soros has indicated, it can be argued that China saved the Euro in its direst moment in its short history. The first part of this paper presents evidence to support this thesis. Both by articulating a public relations campaign of support through public statements and *Xinhua* commentaries to counterbalance Euro-scaremongering coming of the Anglo-American press and by claiming to buy and actually buying debt from cash-strapped Eurozone peripheral countries, the Chinese leadership had considerable influence in maintaining the market value and credibility of the European currency. While the buying of European debt by China has been widely reported in the press and is now one of the main research topics in scholarly work focused on EU-China relations, little attention has been given to how China has also helped to stabilise the market value of the Euro by steering market sentiment in favour of the single currency through the effective use of communication and information channels. Paradigmatic of this is SAFE's public communiqué denying a *Financial Times* report claiming that China was considering reducing the share of its reserves in Euros. This is one of the first times ever that SAFE has reacted to news appearing in the press.

What explains this Euro support by China? Several reasons have been highlighted. China wants a strong and united Europe for international and domestic considerations. Internationally, China favours a multipolar world order, and in this imaginary scenario Europe should be an important pole. In first instance to counterbalance US power and secondly because it is the region with more experience in supranational coordination and cooperation. Domestically, China wants a strong Europe because a fragmentation of Europe could potentially reinforce regionalist tendencies within China bringing social instability. On the economic side there are powerful reasons for China to support the Euro. China needs to diversify out of the Dollar and it needs to protect its already substantial stock of Euro-denominated assets. With more than $800bn at stake, the Euro has become too big to fail for China. The European market remains vital for China too. The EU is its biggest export destination and the biggest origin of technology. A prolonged crisis in Europe is neither in the interest of the Europeans nor the Chinese. Finally, China is using this opportunity to enhance its image as a responsible power in Europe. China tries to be a good friend. It is here to help but it is also honest in saying that ultimately only Europe can save Europe. While in Europe many think that China is using this crisis to advance in its strategy of 'divide and rule' by pursuing bilateral strategies and playing the European countries off against each other. This appears to be a disingenuous assessment. The truth is that it is Europe that is divided not that China wants to divide it. It is perfectly legitimate that China asks for certain returns if it is helping Europe overcome its deepest crisis in generations. Cooperation in international relations as in everyday life is based on give and take. The crux of the matter is that Europe needs to treat China not only as a market but also as a world power, and it needs to be aware that if it wants to be a strong and assertive partner it needs to speak with one voice. Until Europe does not achieve that it will always distrust China not out of China's strengths but rather more because of Europe's weaknesses.

References

Allen, P. (2010) 'George Soros Is right, the Euro May Be Doomed', *CNBC News*, 15 April.

Anderlini, J. and T. Alloway (2011) 'Trade reveal China shift from Dollar', *Financial Times*, 20 June.

Anderlini, J. and D. Oakley (2010) 'China fund "very concerned" on shaky Eurozone', *Financial Times*, 27 May.

Baldwin, R. and C. Wyplosz (2010) 'How to destroy the Eurozone: Feldstein's Euro-holiday idea', VoxEU, 22 February.
Blanchard, B. (2011) 'China confident Europe can handle debt crisis', *Reuters*, 20 October.
Buckley, C. (2012) 'Wen says China has stake in helping Europe', *Reuters*, 5 February.
Dennis, N. (2010) 'China pension fund comments boost the Euro', *Financial Times*, 10 June.
Eichengreen, B. (2007) 'The Breakup of the Euro Area', Working Paper No. 13393, National Bureau of Economic Research (NBER), Cambridge, September.
Eichengreen, B. (2009) 'The Crisis and the Euro', Working Paper 23, Royal Elcano Institute, Madrid, 14 May.
Eichengreen, B. (2011) *Exorbitant Privilege: The Rise and Fall of the Dollar*, Oxford and New York, Oxford University Press.
Feldstein, M. (2010) 'Let Greece take a Eurozone "holiday"', *Financial Times*, 16 February.
Godement. F., J. Parello-Plesner and A. Richard (2011) 'The Scramble for Europe', Policy Brief ECFR 37, European Council on Foreign Relations, July.
Grajewski, M. and P. Taylor (2010) 'EU urges China to let yuan rise faster, Wen demurs', *Reuters*, 5 October.
Handelsblatt (2010) 'Anleihenmarkt: China reicht Griechenland helfende Hand' (Bond market: China extends helping hand to Greece), 2 October.
Harui, R. (2010) 'Bootle Says Euro May Be at "Early Stages" of Breakup', *Bloomberg News*, 24 March.
Heaney, V. (2010) 'Now Eurozone doubts are mainstream', *Financial Times*, July 4.
Jian, J. (2009) 'China says "no thanks" to G-2', *Asia Times*, 29 May.
Jonung, L. and E. Drea (2009) 'The Euro: It can't happen. It's a bad idea. It won't last: US economists on the EMU, 1989–2002', Economic Papers No. 395, European Commission, December.
Junquera, N. (2011) 'China comprará más deuda española y pondrá dinero para sanear las cajas' (China will buy more Spanish debt and put more money to revive the cajas), *El País*, 12 April.
Khanna, P. and M. Leonard (2011) 'Why China wants a G-3 World', *New York Times*, 7 September.
Klaus, V. (2010) 'The Euro Zone Has Failed', *Wall Street Journal*, 1 June.
Krugman, P. (2009) 'China's Dollar Trap', *New York Times*, 2 April.
Krugman, P. (2010) 'Europe's OK; the Euro isn't', *New York Times*, 11 January.
Li, L., A. Batson and J. Shaw (2010) 'China Denies Reviewing Euro Holdings', *Wall Street Journal*, 27 May.

Mallet, V. and G. Wiesmann (2011) 'China's Spanish debt buys put at €6bn', *Financial Times*, 6 January.
Ministry of Commerce of China (MoCoC 2002) 'China to Continue Padding Forex Reserves with Euros', 8 January. <http://english.mofcom.gov.cn/aarticle/newsrelease/commonnews/200211/20021100052190.html>.
Oakley, D. and J. Anderlini (2010) 'China reviews Eurozone bold holdings', *Financial Times*, 26 May.
Oakley, D. and A. Sakoui (2010) 'China offers Spain €1bn confidence vote', *Financial Times*, 12 July.
Orlik, T. and B. Davis (2012) 'Beijing Diversifies Away From U. S. Dollar', *Wall Street Journal*, 2 March.
Pulliam, S., K. Kelly and C. Mollenkamp (2010) 'Hedge Funds Try "Career Trade" Against Euro', *Wall Street Journal*, 26 February.
Qin, Y. (2009) Interview with the author, China Foreign Affairs University, Beijing, 13 May.
Rachman, G. (2010) 'How Germany could come to kill the Euro', *Financial Times*, 22 November.
Reuters (2010) 'China offers rare glimpse into reserves, heavy in Dollars', 3 September.
Sender, H. (2011) 'China has much to gain from supporting the Euro', *Financial Times*, 3 February.
Shambaugh, D. (2008) 'China eyes Europe in the world: real convergence or cognitive dissonance', in D. Shambaugh, E. Sandschneider and H. Zhou (eds) *China-Europe Relations: Perceptions, Policies and Prospects*, Abingdon, New York, Routledge, 127–47.
Song, X. (2010) 'European "models" and their implications to China: internal and external perspectives', *Review of International Studies*, 36, 755–75.
Tang, J. (1999) 'Asia and Europe Work Together to Create a Better Future', Speech delivered to the Second ASEM Foreign Minister's Meeting, Berlin, 29 March.
Vermeiren, M. (2011) 'Monetary Power and Europe: European Autonomy in the Global Monetary System', paper presented at the Annual Conference of the British International Studies Association (BISA), Manchester, 27–29 April.
Wang, X. and C. Liu (2012) 'Show of confidence in Europe', *China Daily*, 13 March.
Wee, S.-L. (2011) 'China says Europe will overcome debt crisis', *Reuters*, 6 November.
Wen, J. (2005) 'Strengthening ASEM Economic and Financial Cooperation to Promote Common Development', Speech at the Openening Ceremony of the Sixth ASEM Finance Ministers' Meeting, Tianjin, 26 June.
White, G. (2010) 'Soros: China Saved the Euro', *Reuters*, 15 September.
Wise, P. (2010) 'Portugal gains on China's appetite for debt', *Financial Times*, 28 October.

Wu, L. (2011) 'Commentary: Time for EU to recognize China's market economy status', *Xinhua*, 14 September.

Xie, A. (2011) 'China should not save Europe', *China.org.cn*, 3 December.

Xinhua (2005) 'Not much "hot money" in China: top banker', 8 March.

Xinhua (2007) 'China's deputy central banker predicts bigger share of the Euro in world reserves', 31 May.

Xinhua (2010) 'Euro will not fail', 29 November.

Xinhua (2011) 'China is a friend indeed for debt-ridden Europe', 30 October.

Xu, M. (2007) 'The Euro and Its Implication to East Asia', in L. Dong and G. Heiduk (eds) *The EU's Experience in Integration: A model for ASEAN+3?* Bern, Peter Lang, 273–96.

Yu, Y. (2009) Interview with the author, Institute of World Economics and Politics, Chinese Academy of Social Sciences, Beijing, 27 April 2009.

Zachariahs, C. and R. Harui (2010) 'China Favors Euro Over Dollars as Bernanke Alters Path', *Bloomberg News*, 16 August.

Zhou, H. (2009), Interview with the author, Institute of European Studies, CASS headquarters, Beijing, 23 April 2009.

Zhou, X. (2009a) 'Reform of the International Monetary System', Speeches, People's Bank of China, 23 March <http://www.pbc.gov.cn/english/detail.asp?col=6500&id=178>.

Zhu, L. (2008) 'Chinese perceptions of the EU and the China-Europe relationship', in D. Shambaugh, E. Sandschneider and H. Zhou (eds) *China-Europe Relations: Perceptions, Policies and Prospects*, New York, Routledge, 148–73.

JOHN RYAN

5 Alan Greenspan and the Decline of the Federal Reserve's Dollar Policy

Introduction

The US Dollar has probably been the closest thing to a true global currency that the world has ever seen. For decades, the use of the US Dollar has been absolutely dominant in international trade. This has been beneficial for the US financial system and for US consumers, and it has given the US government tremendous power and influence around the globe. That privilege now is not only 'exorbitant' but 'extortionate'. How long the rest of the world can allow the US to exercise this extortionate privilege is uncertain.

The US Dollar is gradually losing reserve currency status which has been blamed on the policies of the Greenspan and Bernanke Federal Reserve. The Federal Reserve's quantitative easing has undermined the credibility of US financial diplomacy and has been seen as a welfare system for large asset holders. Take the concerned German reaction to the Fed's massive quantitative easing plan as an example. Finance minister Wolfgang Schäuble commented, 'With all due respect, US policy is clueless.' Schäuble said the issues that the Fed's policy attempts to address are not the country's fundamental problems. Quantitative easing is designed to lower interest rates: it makes the yield on treasury bonds go down, and then lower rates spread, in theory, to the rest of the economy. In Schäuble's words, it promotes liquidity, or the ease with which money moves around. It also promotes inflation, which, like low interest rates, theoretically encourages people to spend money now.[1]

1 *Reuters*, 'Global anger swells at Fed actions', 5 November 2010.

The US Dollar's resilience has been questioned at least three times in the post-war era – in the 1960s as gold reserves ran short, amid Japan's rise in the 1980s, and during the emergence of the Euro in the late 1990s. The US Dollar has always rebounded in a reflection of US economic prowess. Unrivalled liquidity and stability of US financial markets and scale are benefits of the US Dollar in global transactions.[2]

The importance of the US Dollar's predominance in global trade cannot be over-stated. Being the major global reserve currency supports the US Dollar even though the US keeps borrowing and expanding its money supply. So the US is acutely sensitive to any signs that such reserve currency status is under threat.[3] And some concrete challenges are emerging especially from China.

How Greenspan destroyed the American dream

The policy of the Federal Reserve provides a particularly good example of the mistakes a central bank can make with regard to financial crises. The Federal Reserve promoted hasty liberalisation and gave up an effective supervision over financial institutions. Moreover, 'Greenspan's doctrine' which opposed any reaction to the build-up of asset price bubbles went hand in hand with big and lasting reductions of interest rates after each time a bubble had burst; for example, policy easing after the crisis of Long Term Capital Management in the late 1990s which fed the dot.com bubble. In 2000 the bursting of the dot.com bubble also made the Federal Reserve lower its interest rates in the years 2001–4 which can be considered as an

2 Suominen, Kati (2010), 'The dollar question: Where are we?', 9 July, Voxeu.org.

3 Ryan, John (2012), 'The Dollar: Exorbitant or Extortionate Privilege?', *Social Europe*, 26 April.

important factor behind the build-up of imbalances unveiled during the subprime crisis.[4]

The Federal Reserve regional banks are quasi-public and quasi-private entities owned by member banks. The New York Fed, for instance, pays dividends to institutions such as JP Morgan, but has an .org web address. The Reserve banks are governed by Boards of Directors that are drawn mostly from the banking sectors of their regions, as well as large companies and the occasional union leader or university president. Jamie Dimon, Head of JP Morgan, was on the board of the New York Fed when JP Morgan was negotiating with the New York Fed to buy Bear Stearns. The impression of regulatory capture of the Federal Reserve by Wall Street banks is given more credence by these types of relationships.[5]

The problem for this Federal Reserve System is a lack of democratic accountability.

The regional Federal Reserve banks still appoint their own regulators. Dividends go directly from the Reserve banks to private banks; the lack of ethics and the corruption of the macro-economics profession at the heart of the Federal Reserve's research imperatives have left its credibility seriously in doubt.[6]

Unfortunately, the concept of academic and political independence is just a concept and does not align itself to the reality of the Federal Reserve policy operations. The Fed also has a large research staff, and funds most macro-economic monetary policy research. It is difficult to find high profile economists in monetary policy who have no financial ties to the Federal Reserve banks.[7]

4 Ryan, John, and Adam Koronowski (2009), 'Greenspan's Legacy and Bernanke's attitude to the Financial Crisis', in Department of Economics, Ca' Foscari University of Venice, Working Paper series No. 19, September.

5 Stoller, Matt (2010), 'Suddenly Everyone's Talking about How Our Money Works – Is it Time to End the Fed?', New Deal 2.0, 2 *December*.

6 Stoller, Matt (2010), 'Suddenly Everyone's Talking about How Our Money Works – Is it Time to End the Fed?', New Deal 2.0, 2 *December*.

7 Stoller, Matt (2010), 'Suddenly Everyone's Talking about How Our Money Works – Is it Time to End the Fed?', New Deal 2.0, 2 *December*.

The assumptions of continued US Dollar supremacy are deeply hubristic in the more or less exact meaning of that word: an overbearing self-confidence that leads to ruin. And with hubris comes ex post denial, as events and one's personal role within them are rewritten to accommodate emerging realities. Greenspan's assumption that markets know best and that tough regulation is unnecessary and the political belief in the social value of growth in financial services have not disappeared because they are deeply engrained ideologically and institutionally.[8]

Greenspan's Federal Reserve responsibility for subprime collapse

The Federal Reserve and Greenspan's leadership bear blame for the subprime collapse and the wider damage caused by the ongoing crisis in the US. As is becoming ever more apparent, many of the lending practices in the mortgage market during these years, especially in the subprime market, involved carelessness, deception, or both. Many people borrowed who had no prospect of servicing the loans they took out; they were hoping either to resell the house at a higher price, or to refinance it and draw on the appreciated value to make their payments. Some borrowers were apparently induced to buy houses they could not afford, or to take out loans they should not have been granted, by irresponsible brokers and other agents keen to make commissions on transactions despite knowing they were inappropriate.[9]

8 Engelen, Ewald, Ismail Erturk, Julie Froud, Sukhdev Johal, Adam Leaver, Michael Moran and Karel Williams (2011), 'Misrule of experts? The financial crisis as elite debacle', Centre for Research on Socio-Cultural Change Working Paper No. 94, March.

9 Greenspan, Alan (2007), *The Age of Turbulence: Adventures in a New World*, Penguin.

Many of the banks that packaged these loans into securities also put them into complex investment vehicles that they did not understand, and sold them to investors who understood even less about them. The credit rating agencies which investors normally relied on to inform them of such risks were at best useless.[10] The wreckage consists of abandoned houses, defaulted loans and displaced homeowners.[11] With respect to the housing bubble, the Federal Reserve asserts its innocence. It says that its monetary policy was appropriate. It also takes the position that while, ex post, it is clear that supervision and regulation was too lax, no one saw the housing and credit bubble forming. Consequently, they cannot be blamed.[12]

The assertion that the stance of monetary policy was appropriate given the measured inflation rate just assumes away the problem. If policy contributed to the bubble, then it was inappropriate regardless of the inflation rate. Contrary to the Federal Reserve position, people did see the housing and credit bubbles forming, although they were in the minority such as Raghuram Rajan,[13] Dean Baker[14] and Joseph Stiglitz.[15]

Most importantly, the Federal Reserve as the central bank and the principal banking regulator alone had the responsibility of forestalling systemic risks. Even if no one else saw the bubble forming, the Fed should

10 John Ryan, 'The Negative Impact of Credit Rating Agencies and proposals for better regulation', *Stiftung Wissenschaft und Politik*, European Integration working papers, Berlin, Germany, January 2012.

11 Ryan, John, and Adam Koronowski (2009), 'Greenspan's Legacy and Bernanke's attitude to the Financial Crisis', in Department of Economics, Ca' Foscari University of Venice, Working Paper series No. 19, September.

12 Ryan, John, and Adam Koronowski (2009), 'Greenspan's Legacy and Bernanke's attitude to the Financial Crisis', in Department of Economics, Ca' Foscari University of Venice, Working Paper series No. 19, September.

13 Rajan, Raghuram G. (2005), 'Has Financial Development Made the World Riskier?', Federal Reserve Bank of Kansas City, Jackson Hole, Wyoming, 27 August.

14 Baker, Dean (2002), 'The Run Up in Home Prices: Is It Real or Is It Another Bubble?', August 5, <www.cepr.net/documents/publications/housing_2002_08.htm>.

15 Stiglitz, Joseph (2006), 'Economic Crisis or Global Malaise in 2006?', The Economists' Voice Volume, Issue 2.

have. Saying no one else saw the crisis brewing is no defence and is not accurate.[16]

Bernanke was also a proponent of the 'Asian Savings Glut' theory which puts much of the blame for global imbalances at Asia's doorstep and exonerates over-consumption by US citizens for a credit crisis which began in America, the so-called 'Blame Asia' game. While there may be excess savings, it is disingenuous to blame Asia for problems created in the United States. Bernanke, like Greenspan, is an ultra-free market libertarian who believes markets always are better informed than regulators. This takes libertarian views to an extreme which Stephen Roach has called 'Deregulation as Crony Capitalism'. He sees a more nuanced belief in free markets as more appropriate.[17]

The Federal Reserve, Securities and Exchange Commission (SEC), Federal Deposit Insurance Corporation, the Office of the Comptroller of the Currency, and the Office of Thrift Supervision were at best incompetent and at worse captive to the companies they are supposed to regulate. As Harry Markopolos would later testify before Congress, 'The SEC roars like a mouse and bites like a flea'.[18]

Top officials at the US Federal Reserve took months to realise the 2007 financial crisis would rock the world's largest economy, according to an embarrassing set of meeting transcripts released on 18 January 2013.[19] The transcripts reveal that some Fed policy makers even viewed the crisis, which erupted in August 2007 on the back of problems in the market for subprime mortgage loans, as good news because markets were pricing in more risk. The minutes of the Federal Open Market Committee's (FOMC) 2007 meetings, which are released with a five-year delay, raise the question

16 Ryan, John (2009a), 'The Greenspan Federal Reserve Role in the Financial Crisis' in Department of Economics, Ca' Foscari University of Venice, Working Paper series No. 4, February.

17 Roach, Stephen (2009), 'The case against Bernanke', *Financial Times*, 26 August.

18 Markopolos, Harry (2010), *No One Would Listen: A True Financial Thriller*, John Wiley & Sons.

19 'Fed minutes show slow crisis reaction', 19 January 2013, *Financial Times*.

of whether the recession would have been less severe if the Fed had reacted faster instead of continuing to forecast steady growth.[20]

On 7 August 2007 two days before the European Central Bank (ECB) made its unprecedented offer of unlimited funds to Eurozone banks to counter a severe liquidity shortage, Frederic Mishkin, then a governor at the Federal Reserve Board, described the subprime crisis as 'Basically what I think is happening in a way is quite a good thing: We were concerned that the markets were a little too optimistic, that there was too much opacity, and that people weren't worried about it,' Mishkin said. 'Now, in fact, they are worried about it, and I think that is fundamentally a healthy situation'. A day after the ECB's offer of unlimited funds, on 10 August, US Treasury secretary Timothy Geithner, then president of the New York Fed, said there was 'no indication from any of our counterparts yet that any major institutions face a significant funding or solvency issue'.[21]

Earlier in May 2007, Donald Kohn, then vice-chair of the Fed, had said there was little to suggest problems in the subprime market would spread to other credit markets. 'I think we've seen enough since the subprime problems started to be pretty sure that the risk is no more than the normal kind,' Kohn said.[22]

Ben Bernanke, chair of the Federal Reserve, said at the same meeting: 'It's a question of market functioning, not a question of bailing anyone out.' Bernanke underestimated the risks of a looming financial blow-up. 'I do not expect insolvency or near insolvency among major financial institutions,' he said in December 2007. The crisis in the market for subprime loans set off a series of events that eventually led to the collapse of US investment banks Bear Stearns and Lehman Brothers.[23]

By December 2007, some Fed officials had begun to recognise very late the scale of the problem they were facing. At the FOMC's meeting on 11 December 2007, Janet Yellen, then president of the San Francisco Fed

20 'Fed minutes show slow crisis reaction', 19 January 2013, *Financial Times*.
21 'Fed minutes show slow crisis reaction', 19 January 2013, *Financial Times*.
22 'Fed minutes show slow crisis reaction', 19 January 2013, *Financial Times*.
23 'Fed minutes show slow crisis reaction', 19 January 2013, *Financial Times*.

and one of the first committee members to understand the potential severity of the developing crisis, said: 'The bad news since our last meeting has grown steadier and louder, as strains in financial markets have resurfaced and intensified and as the economy has shown clear signs of faltering.' She added: 'The possibilities of a credit crunch developing and of the economy slipping into a recession seem all too real.'[24]

Nevertheless Yellen's foresight is being hugely exaggerated. For instance, the mainstream media is touting the idea that she was one of the economists who recognised that there was a housing bubble forming. A read of FOMC minutes shows no such thing. The most she did was consider the idea that housing prices might be too high. She missed the bubble, just like everyone else in the Federal Reserve. In fact, Yellen in October 2005, at the height of the housing bubble, delivered a speech effectively proposing that monetary policy could mitigate any negative economic consequences of a housing collapse, and arguing that the Fed had no role in preventing further housing risk distortions: 'First, if the bubble were to deflate on its own, would the effect on the economy be exceedingly large? Second, is it unlikely that the Fed could mitigate the consequences? Third, is monetary policy the best tool to use to deflate a house-price bubble? My answers to these questions in the shortest possible form are, "no, no and no".'[25]

Greenspan – Don't blame me

In March 2010 Alan Greenspan published a paper with the aim to justify his policies and avoid any responsibility for failures during his terms of office as chairman of the Federal Reserve. Greenspan's paper argues that a global housing bubble was primarily caused by a sharp drop

24 'Fed minutes show slow crisis reaction', 19 January 2013, *Financial Times*.

25 Epstein, Ethan (2013), 'Did Janet Yellen predict the recession?', *The Weekly Standard*, 31 July.

in long-term interest rates from 2000 to 2005, brought about by export-oriented growth in developing economies, especially China, after the end of the Cold War. China, saving the US Dollars it was earning, in effect made money available for cheap loans. 'In short, geopolitical events ultimately led to a fall in long-term mortgage interest rates that in turn led, with a lag, to the unsustainable boom in house prices globally,' he wrote. Greenspan also tried to refute, or at least deflect, the criticism he has received for the Federal Reserve conduct of monetary policy in the years after the burst of the dot.com bubble in 2001 and the subsequent recession.[26]

'Almost all market participants of my acquaintance were aware of the growing risks, but also cognisant that risk had often remained underpriced for years. I raised the problem of "irrational exuberance" in 1996 only to watch the dotcom boom, after a one-day stumble, continue to inflate for four more years, unrestrained by a cumulative increase of 350 basis points in the federal funds rate from 1994 to 2000. Similarly in 2002, I expressed my concerns before the Federal Open Market Committee that "... our extraordinary housing boom ... financed by very large increases in mortgage debt – cannot continue indefinitely." It lasted until 2006. The former Fed chairman also acknowledged that the Federal Reserve failed to grasp the magnitude of the housing bubble but argued, as he had before, that its policy of low interest rates was not to blame.'[27]

The US Public Broadcasting Service *Frontline* documentary showed how powerful regulators and policymakers thwarted efforts to make the market of Credit Default Swaps (CDS) more transparent. The Fed (under Alan Greenspan), the Treasury (under Robert Rubin and then Larry Summers), and the SEC (under Arthur Levitt) prevented attempts by Brooksley Born of the Commodity Future Trading Commission (CFTC) to shed light on the multi-trillion Dollar Over-the-counter (OTC)

26 Greenspan, Alan (2010a), 'The Crisis', Greenspan Associates LLC, Second Draft: 9 March.

27 Greenspan, Alan (2010b), 'Testimony to Financial Crisis Inquiry Commission', Wednesday, 7 April.

derivatives market, which included credit default swaps, at the end of the 1990s. Greenspan led the effects to force regulator Born to resign.[28] Just in time for his next and final act as Federal Reserve chairman: from 2001–4, Greenspan pumped up the biggest housing bubble in human history by holding interest rates close to zero, while touring the country promoting subprime mortgages. Then in late 2005, when the bubble was ready to burst, Greenspan tendered his resignation and switched over to the other side, signing lucrative contracts with three investment firms all of which took positions against American homeowners, and earned billions. First, Greenspan signed up to work for Deutsche Bank, which was sued for securities fraud for selling an Abacus-like CDO to a Warren Buffett-owned bank, M&T; Greenspan also worked for Pimco, which earned $2 billion in a single day in September 2008, when Fannie Mae and Freddie Mac were nationalised with Greenspan's lobbying help; and lastly, Greenspan went to work for Paulson & Co., the hedge fund that raked in $1 billion off the same Abacus CDO deal that brought the SEC fraud suit against Goldman Sachs.[29]

It is forgotten now that in 1984, Alan Greenspan was hired by the most notorious criminal in the savings and loan racket: Charles Keating. Keating laundered money through Lincoln Savings & Loan. He needed someone to write a letter to his regulator, [the Federal Home Loan Bank of San Francisco] that stated Lincoln Savings & Loan's investments were sound. In 1985, Greenspan wrote to the Federal Home Loan Bank that Lincoln's management 'is seasoned and expert in selecting and making direct investments'. By that time, Lincoln was not only loaded up with deals through Michael Milken junk bond trader,[30] it was swapping them at a profit with its holding company, American Continental Corporation. American Continental Corporation – and Charles Keating – had been

28 Public Broadcasting Service (PBS) (2009), *Frontline*, 'The Warning: Who Knew About the Looming Financial Crisis?'

29 Ames, Mark (2010), '10 Ways the American Economy Is Built on Fraud', Exiled online, 29 April.

30 Stein, Benjamin (1992), *License to Steal: The Untold Story of Michael Milken and the Conspiracy to Bilk the Nation*, Simon & Schuster.

spun out of Carl Lindner's American Financial Corporation. Keating was known as Lindner's hatchet man. [In 1978, Keating had offered no defence when the SEC charged him – in the words of Martin Mayer – with: 'arranging fraudulent loans to himself ... from a bank owned by his friend and employer Carl Lindner.'] Greenspan surely knew who he was dealing with. He had been on Wall Street in the 1960s.[31]

In the 1980s, Greenspan must have known Lincoln was part of the Riklis, Steinberg, Lindner, Boesky, Milken group. Greenspan in 1984–5 worked as a lobbyist for Charles Keating trying to push regulators off his back and vouching on the record for Keating's character. Keating was eventually jailed for fraud in one of the worst savings and loan collapses.[32] This poses serious questions over Greenspan's commercial acumen, lack of ethical compass, poor policy understanding and poor judgment which should have been warning signs for the future. These serious issues were either ignored or forgotten.

Greenspan had not revealed services rendered to Lincoln Savings & Loan. Greenspan slipped Lincoln Savings & Loan into the side pocket of 'advocacy projects'. Senator Proxmire lectured nominee Greenspan for the Fed chairmanship: 'As chairman of the Federal Reserve you play the key role in approval or disapproval of these massive bank mergers ... I would feel much better about this appointment if there was somewhere in your record an indication of your awareness of the dangers to our economy of excessive financial concentration'.[33]

In 1989, the Federal Reserve permitted JP Morgan, of which Greenspan had been director before becoming Fed chairman, to underwrite Xerox debt. This was the first such debt issue from a commercial bank since 1933,

31 Sheehan, Frederick J. (2010b), 'Chairman Greenspan: A Fiat Mind for a Fiat Age', *Mises Daily* 15 June.

32 Sheehan, Frederick J. (2010a), A speech delivered at the Ludwig von Mises Institute Conference: 'Austrian Economics and the Financial Markets', held at the University Club in New York City, 22 May.

33 Sheehan, Frederick J. (2010a), A speech delivered at the Ludwig von Mises Institute Conference: 'Austrian Economics and the Financial Markets', held at the University Club in New York City, 22 May.

the year of the Glass-Steagall Act. In 1990, the Federal Reserve permitted JP Morgan to underwrite stock. *Time* magazine called this 'the widest breach of Glass-Steagall yet'.[34]

Greenspan was testifying to the Financial Crisis Inquiry Commission[35] eager to portray himself as an innocent bystander to forces beyond his control. In his rewriting of history, his clout in Washington was so slight that he was ineffectual at 'influencing the Congress'. The 'roots' of the crisis, he lectured, dated back to the fall of the Berlin Wall in 1989. In other words: Wherever the blame ends, it does not end with the former Fed Reserve Chairman.

As he has previously said in defending his inability to spot the colossal bubble, 'Everybody missed it – academia, the Federal Reserve, all regulators'.[36]

Michael Burry, an investor chronicled in the book *The Big Short* by Michael Lewis told in detail of how Greenspan and others in power 'either wilfully or ignorantly aided or abetted the reckless boom and the ensuing bust'. When 'mistakes are made' they are always made by someone else.[37]

The relationship between Greenspan, US politicians, and the press was not dissimilar to the rise of Chauncey Gardner in Jerzy Kosinski's 1979 film *Being There*. Chauncey is a slow minded gardener whose only recreational activity is watching TV. Greenspan was said to watch CNBC in his office. Chauncey becomes a mystical seer in Washington. His fame rising, he meets the president. Chauncey tells him that growth in the garden comes in the spring and summer, but then we have fall and winter. 'As long as the roots are not severed all is well and will be well again.' The president interprets

34 Sheehan, Frederick J. (2010a), A speech delivered at the Ludwig von Mises Institute Conference: 'Austrian Economics and the Financial Markets', held at the University Club in New York City, 22 May.

35 'The Financial Crisis Inquiry Report', Financial Crisis Inquiry Commission, January 2011.

36 Greenspan, Alan (2010b), Testimony to Financial Crisis Inquiry Commission, Wednesday, 7 April.

37 Lewis, Michael (2010), 'The Big Short: Inside the Doomsday Machine', Allen Lane.

this to be an economic forecast, and he 'must admit ... (It) is one of the most refreshing and optimistic statements I've heard in a very, very long time'.[38]

The parallel is of a man who mesmerised large pockets of seemingly intelligent people, not by any complete thought, but by phrases and words, such as 'irrational exuberance', 'conundrum', 'measured', 'soft spot', and 'productivity', his forecasting record was abysmal, yet his face would adorn the front pages of newspapers the day after he issued another meandering statement. As the Fed continued to lose control of money, Greenspan monetary policy seemed to be all that mattered. As his forecasts grew worse, he moved markets all the more. Greenspan succeeded in a visual culture that was limited to short bursts of attention and limited memories.[39]

Conclusions

A more thorough analysis of the Fed's monetary stance is provided by William White, former head of research at the Bank for International Settlements. White starts by observing what just about everyone in the world – with the notable exception of the current Fed chairman – acknowledges, that the Fed's easy money policy after the dot.com debacle resulted in reckless credit expansion, the inflation of housing bubbles around the world and the appearance of an overly leveraged and opaque shadow banking system.[40]

38 Sheehan, Frederick J. (2009), 'Panderer to Power: The True Story of How Alan Greenspan Enriched Wall Street and Left a Legacy of Recession', McGraw-Hill Professional.

39 Sheehan, Frederick J. (2009), 'Panderer to Power: The True Story of How Alan Greenspan Enriched Wall Street and Left a Legacy of Recession', McGraw-Hill Professional.

40 White, William R. (2012), 'Ultra Easy Monetary Policy and the Law of Unintended Consequences', Dallas Fed, August.

White observes that leveraged speculators have been the prime beneficiaries of the Greenspan/Bernanke era of easy money. Prudent savers, on the other hand, suffer from negative real returns on their cash and fixed income investments. Bernanke's low rates are delivering what Keynes gleefully termed the 'euthanasia of the rentier class'. Low rates have not even brought enduring benefits to the least advantaged, who have suffered most from the housing crisis and from subsequent high levels of unemployment. The distribution of economic spoils has become unfair.[41]

The Federal Reserve has been instrumental especially under Alan Greenspan in stripping away the regulations that had been so important in ensuring a reasonably stable global financial system. Greenspan's reputation has suffered from two big mistakes. The first was his failure to see the importance of the subprime housing bubble and the dangerous vulnerability of the financial mechanism that supported it. The second was his deep-seated conviction that the unregulated financial system was self-stabilising. So he promoted deregulation and financial consolidation and, when this simple faith proved wrong, allowed disaster to strike. Hindsight leaves no doubt that it would have been a good idea to prick the housing bubble. Instead Fed policy turned into a case of bad ideas coming home to roost. Greenspan, as a prominent opponent of financial regulation put the US Dollar on the road to decline.

It may even be that QE has actually had a negative effect on employment, recovery and economic activity.

This is because the only notable effect QE is having is to raise asset prices. If the so-called wealth effect – of higher stock indices and property markets combined with lower interest rates – has failed to generate a sustained rebound in demand for private borrowing, then the higher asset values can start to depress economic activity. Just think of a property market where unclear job or income prospects make consumers nervous about borrowing but house prices keep going up. The higher prices may

41 White, William R. (2012), 'Ultra Easy Monetary Policy and the Law of Unintended Consequences', Dallas Fed, August.

act as either a deterrent or a bar to market entry, such as when first time buyers are unable to afford to step onto the property ladder.

This is the exact opposite of the Fed's beliefs, that the wealth effect encourages people to spend more. But what we saw in the cycle just past was that the spending consisted to a significant degree of tapping into accumulated paper wealth through borrowing. This wasn't spending more out of discretionary income out of confidence; this was to a significant degree monetising housing assets. And the value of those assets proved to be a hell of a lot more volatile than the Fed dreamed.

Conclusion

A reserve currency has to be stable to be effective. It is becoming apparent that the US Dollar is gradually losing the confidence of global markets. Since the financial crisis the Dollar privilege is not only 'exorbitant' but 'extortionate'. Countries such as China are not willing to allow the US to exercise this extortionate privilege unconditionally.

The potential geopolitical implications of a Dollar decline are immense. The US would lose its privileged seigniorage position and with that the ability to achieve permanently higher returns on foreign assets than the returns paid to foreigners who invest in the US. So as the reign of the US Dollar as the world reserve currency is definitely being threatened, the shift in international trade is going to have massive implications for the US economy. Due to failures in Federal Reserve policymaking and the reckless accumulation of debt by the US government, the status of the US Dollar as the reserve currency of the world is now in decline.

The US Dollar has been used as an exorbitant privilege to further its geopolitical objectives. The Dollar's primacy enables the US government and households to accumulate debts on a scale that in other countries would risk a crisis of creditor confidence. By being allowed to live beyond its means, the US can therefore more readily afford the armed forces that underpin its global role. This clout in turn enables the US to shift the onus of adjusting macroeconomic imbalances on the others, especially allies such as Japan for whom allegiance to the Dollar is a tacit quid pro quo for US military protection.

The Dollar's dominance of international finance confers a further power that is unique to the United States. Because all Dollar payments are cleared through the Federal Reserve, the US can threaten to cut off any financial institution dealing with a country that is the target of international sanctions. This capacity to enforce a financial blockade, such as the one in place against Iran, is the principal way in which US power is enhanced by virtue of the Dollar's widespread private use.

China's proposal would have members surrender part of their reserves to the IMF in exchange for SDRs, effectively making the IMF a global vault. The benefit here would be simply one of diversification – the IMF would have no enforcement authority in the management of global liquidity beyond its current one. The use of an SDR in international trade and finance is painfully slow. Therefore SDR is unlikely to be a practical alternative to the US Dollar. The prospects of other currencies challenging the Dollar's primacy specifically the Euro and the Renminbi, have major challenges to address if they seek to rival the Dollar's powerful financial diplomacy. China which has made progress towards the internationalisation of its currency, is often regarded as the most likely future contender in the international monetary system. The Euro also has been billed as a candidate to weaken Dollar hegemony. But the recent Eurozone crisis which still has not been resolved has undermined the Euro's prospects. Realistically the Euro is a regional currency which will probably be a major player in a multi-polar currency system. Both China and the European Union have long argued for a more multi-polar monetary system and actions of the Greenspan and Bernanke Fed have led to a revival of these calls.

On the economic side there are powerful reasons for China to support the Euro. China needs to diversify out of the Dollar and it needs to protect its already substantial stock of Euro-denominated assets. The European market remains vital for China too. The EU is its biggest export destination and the biggest origin of technology.

The consensus is that it is only a matter of time before the Renminbi becomes an international currency, if not an important reserve currency. The internationalisation of the currency will be an integral part of the leadership's economic reform agenda. In comparison, the Euro is a currency without a state, the challenge that the Renminbi could pose is much more significant from a geopolitical perspective. The sheer size of China's economy certainly helps the Renminbi's internationalisation. Nevertheless, obstacles must be overcome if the Renminbi is to become more than a currency for trade invoicing and is to account for a sizeable share of the central banks' reserves. To create deep, liquid and trusted government bond markets the ruling Communist Party would have to liberalise China's financial markets and largely remove capital controls. In doing so, the Party would deprive itself of the economic tools on which it has relied to buttress its monopoly of political power.

When almost ten years of relative ease for the EMU's single currency came to an abrupt end with the start of the Greek debt crisis in 2010, the debate over the Euro's sustainability quickly turned to the question of whether there can be a monetary union without some sort of fiscal union. The EMU was an enormous undertaking, and it continues to work toward ensuring European price stability among members by integrating monetary systems and by means of a major cross-national currency, the Euro. EMU has grown and evolved, the lack of coordination in policymaking, complex decision-making, and the sheer number of interrelationships between monetary and economic variables have led to serious problems.

Design flaws in the Eurozone were well known from its inception – including a lack of fiscal union and no mechanisms to deal with asymmetric shocks, and diverging competitiveness. However, political imperatives trumped economic concerns in the creation of a united states of Europe, and the Euro was the showpiece of this political project. The Euro will have an important role to play in the multi-polar currency order if the Eurozone draws the right lessons from its ongoing development.

Notes on Contributors

DR MIGUEL OTERO-IGLESIAS is Senior Analyst for the European Economy and Emerging Markets at the Elcano Royal Institute in Madrid and Research Fellow at the Centre for European Integration at ESSCA School of Management in Paris. He is a regular visiting scholar to the Institute of World Economics and Politics at the Chinese Academy of Social Sciences in Beijing. Previously he was research fellow at the Centre for International Studies at the London School of Economics and Political Science and Adjunct Lecturer for Queen Elizabeth House at Oxford University. His main area of research is the international political economy of money and finance, focusing particularly on European and international monetary affairs. He is the author of the book *The Euro, the Dollar and the Global Financial Crisis*.

DR MARIE-JOSÉ RINALDI-LARRIBE holds a PhD in Economics and graduated from the Institute of Political Science (Sciences Po) of Paris. Professor at the International University of Monaco from 2004 to June 2014, she is now a Professor at EDHEC Business School, in France. Expert in European economics and politics, she published two books and several academic articles on European matters.

Professor JOHN RYAN is Research Associate at the Von Hügel Institute of St Edmund's College, University of Cambridge. Previously he was Head of School at SCMS London, an international campus of SCMS Cochin, India. Professor Ryan was a fellow at the London School of Economics and Political Science Centre for International Studies and the European Integration section of the German Institute for International and Security Affairs, Berlin. Professor Ryan has held senior administrative and academic positions at various business schools and policy institutes. He works as a senior adviser for private and public sector organisations. His current areas of research are: Eurozone crisis, global currencies and credit rating agencies.

Index

FSC
www.fsc.org
MIX
Papier | Fördert gute Waldnutzung
FSC® C083411

Kolibri 360 GmbH
Ferdinand-Jühlke-Straße 7
99095 Erfurt, Deutschland
produktsicherheit@kolibri360.de